RÊVE AMÉRICAIN

AN AMERICAN DREAM

24 Aoút 2019

Greenfield Jones

GREENFIELD JONES

ISBN: 1-4392-4811-7
ISBN-13: 9781439248119

Visit www.booksurge.com to order additional copies.

He was impregnably armoured by his ignorance and his good intentions.

Graham Greene, **The Quiet American**

The difference between kitsch and art, said Jung, is the difference between day dreams and night dreams.

Rust Hills, **The Art of the Novel**

"Plan de Paris à Vol d'Oiseau" was published in *Prairie Schooner*

"Had Silicon Been a Gas" was published in *Kansas Quarterly*

Prologue, or What It All Means

It started when women lost their Season. A redheaded woman sitting on a throne, with the dawn rising behind her, was explaining it to him: it all started when women lost their Season. That much was clear, she said, since insofar as sexual readiness was concerned, there was no difference between human males and non-human males of the moderately intelligent sort. It was the Nurse Jan Gooley who was lecturing him and she was crowned in glory as she sat seated naked on a toilet. She said human females varied from other moderately intelligent females in that they greatly outlived their reproductive years (at least with competent dentistry they did), could copulate face-to-face (though it was not necessary for conception), could have orgasms (also not necessary for conception, but likely to encourage it) and that they had no Season. Before that Seasonless time one male had many females and most males hadn't many or any. Then with the Season gone came marriage, in order to control the rampant sexuality of the human female. (Marriage also made males shape up.) That was the explanation of why human civilization was only a few thousand years old: the Season must have been lost maybe six thousand years back or even somewhat before that.

That much made clear sense to him. It was Anthropology – which was Poetry that pretended to be Science. Vonnegut, he would later learn, would confirm that, but probably Kurt meant Fiction and not Poetry. Science Fiction can exist and Vonnegut wrote it. But Science Poetry? An oxymoron of the first order! Imagine a Mensan who wrote Poetry (!), they who regard Poetry as irrational when really it is non- or supra-rational. If he had a taste for it, a Science Fiction writer could start a new religion. But a poet would have no taste for that.

Sci Fi really is neither Science nor Fiction, though neither is Social Science scientific – too many uncontrollable variables to be Science. And probably it's not Social. Ah, but Anthropology! Great fun! Practitioners thereof may make up drôle stories and pretend they are true. (Cf. Margaret Nut-Brown-Skin Mead.) And many laity, on hearing, believe. And perhaps find meaning for and come to base their lives thereupon. New professions arise thereby, with new doctoral programs a certainty. Wars are not out of the question, and many journals are created as well as there being new trends in literary criticism, where aspirants often try to gain a foothold by using the new insights. Insights someone has made up, drawn from thin air and then reinforced with statistics also similarly carefully found. That was so because Men try to formulate the world and stuff it in their socks. But, said Auden, there never was a female colossal silly on the level of Kant or Hegel. (Mead doesn't begin to reach that level.) And, until recently – bless them for it! – no female Chess Grand Masters. What Women do is sacrifice themselves for love, said the redheaded Gooley: we lie to ourselves about it. We are built for it, she said, and our world is smaller and bound by it, she said and smiled. But it is much more intense. We have a much greater stake in Love. She smiled again. Then she flushed.

At last he understood it. But he understood it without stumbling to his desk and writing it down. And the unwritten word is as smoke. (As is the written word, but it takes longer.) So he forgot it all.

I

With the flushing of the toilet in the latrine that joined his and Grisby's BOQ rooms he awoke: he was an Intellectual. He knew: it had been stamped on him. Signed and Certified. Nonetheless when the rushing water sounded Simon could not recall where or who he was. He had dreamt of a red-haired naked woman enveloped in green but it was fading and the only trace left of it was Little Trooper Jude standing rigidly at attention: Simon considered giving him a Dishonorable Discharge but deleted the notion. He opened and then re-shut his eyes. The room in which he lay abed he saw even through closed lids was bleached. It reminded him of the orphanage in winter but the temperature was too high for that and he recalled parachute shrouds were at the windows and that was what made for whiteness and he knew he was in the Air Force. There was a sweet-smelling airborne scent trailing across his bed like a woman's perfume-moistened handkerchief: un mouchoir de poche. French he was thinking in. He was in France. He thought of Jan and her red to auburn hair and cool green eyes. Jan was not an Intellectual.

Which did not mean she was stupid. Being an Intellectual was a Cast and not a Quality of mind and by far most Intelligent people were not Intellectual and any number of Intellectuals were not in the least Intelligent. Mrs Lieutenant Colonel Burger for one – she who often asked *What Does It Mean!* But with an exclamation point and not a question mark. Jan was not like that: few nurses were and those who were Intellectual were best soon out of nursing. Unless they were Spinoza types who did that for their day job so as to leave their nights free for writing philosophy. But never had there been a female colossal silly on the level of Kant or Hegel.

In the shower he picked up razor blades thrown there by the maid who was a Communist and was doing her bit. Perhaps she was an Intellectual since she was French though she was not in a league with Papa Marx whose theories rationalized his Will to Power. Power being something no one in his right mind ever would otherwise allow an Intellectual to have. Thus Spake Professor Shaw (who was his Sociology and Anthropology instructor). Next door was another intelligent non-intellectual: he could hear BM Grisby moving about but apparently he had not yet used the shower in the latrine that joined their rooms since the blades were still on the floor. As a Finance Officer Grisby was content: he was an ROTC boy a Business Major doing his time till he got out and forgot the Air Force and it would all seem a straight line of progression. For Grisby the military was not a hiatus but a time to grow a time to relax a time to put on a bit of experience and his marketability would go up. Grisby talked like that. Be in five figures in a year and six in ten years and then marry well have kids own property then the coronary.

Jan he expected of returning Grisby's veiled interest though he hoped not: but Grisby was not a Catholic and that would be against him. It would be just like Grisby to sign the kids over though and that would be all that Jan would require.

He looked out his door into the DeChirico hallway and saw Dr Shaw in a badly worn black robe bending over to put milk in a saucer for his cat. The professor looked like Lincoln on a hangover except Shaw was taller more intelligent and less handsome. His cat looked like any other alcoholic cat. Shaw's robe seemed to have or to have had gold trim. Raggedy now.

Back in his own room Simon took his clothes garment by garment off the easel he used for a clothes tree. One nice thing about the Military: no tough decisions about what to wear. He stuffed his George Washington pipe for an after-breakfast smoke and looking through their shared latrine to see if Grisby was ready for the walk to the mess hall he saw that a pair of feminine feet stuck out from under the sheet on the bed. Then Grisby shut the door.

He wondered if it was Jan and decided it couldn't be. He tamped his pipe again. It was a good pipe except the face on it was silly: supposedly it was of George Washington and the shop in Paris that sold it had purported visages of Lincoln and Teddy and Jefferson but no matter who it was supposed to be they all looked like the picture of Voltaire in the text from Shaw's U of Maryland class. A true Intellectual was Voltaire who held that every item was susceptible to rational analysis: thus if some item wasn't so susceptible then it didn't exist. Jesuit-trained.

Out in the hall while still waiting for Grisby to finish with the girl in his sack he hopped two-footed from one black square to another. He was the only piece left of an especially bloody chess game. No that could not be since there never was only one piece left: it must be that he was the first to be placed on the board. He supposed he was a Pawn though as a Lieutenant perhaps he could claim Knighthood were it not that his job consisted mainly of signing the Morning Report. It was seldom that one saw the game from a Pawn's-eye-view.

Pawns if asked certainly would say they doubted that they aided at all in the Decision Making Process and probably in their spare time spoke mainly of what they would do Once They Got Out. As for himself he did not intend to get out: like most orphans he found the military familiar and generally he had to admit that it suited him. Shaw had told him that about orphans.

Shaw had offered to teach him chess. The game was one that gave the Illusion of Omnipotence said the Professor. He kept a loaded set on his desk and like Grandmaster Steinmetz had one time challenged God and offered Him Pawn and First Move. In his spare time Simon had been reading up on the game since he had but little else to do so perhaps soon he would accept Shaw's challenge though only as a human.

Grisby locked his door behind himself and they walked out together. For a while it seemed to him that Grisby was the Top American Product: U of Wisconsin from Racine in ROTC and a fraternity. But he formed that opinion before he met Cosmo: Eastern private school too proud to allow national fraternities since it would link them to lesser schools. And only barely tolerate ROTC. Also Cosmo smiled upside down. One learned that in prep school: to hold the lower lip straight and curve the upper one down at the corners so that bottom teeth showed. It was inherited from the Puritans and was a sure and certain sign of Election. Shaw had explained that too.

Jan's smile was American as apple pie. Open. No guile. No irony.

Shaw's cat of a sudden shot between his and Grisby's legs and made a long and misplaced leap at a bird sitting on a crump of weeds. The cat missed not only the bird but the bush too and went into water in the ditch. It sat there. Probably has a hangover said Grisby. It was a very ugly cat indeed which though technically a calico through an unfortunate twist of chromosomes despite its full coat it had come to look as though it had mange.

Shaw gives his cat some drink does he?

Indeed said Grisby: His notion seems to be that he can prove Free Will or the lack of it. If the cat can give it up Shaw thinks maybe *he* can too. Grisby also had talked with the Maryland Professor and took one course for the fun of it. Simon had hardly been to college at all before joining Cadets but was making it with the Maryland program. He said he supposed what Grisby had going with the girl in his room was *de rigueur*. Was she a teacher or a nurse?

Speak English JP speak English. He said it means Happens All the Time. Grisby had small French and made no attempt to pronounce correctly what little he had. Business Administration had not required it. In fairness one had to admit the locals tried no harder to understand his own French than Grisby tried to speak it but made faces and refused to comprehend. Cosmo of course was flawless in his British French. Now there was one who could do the right thing without giving it apparent thought: once Cosmo had worn a double-breasted suit and although no one else had worn one in half a decade Cosmo looked right and the rest of them wrong. Even on this the morning of his coming out he envied Cosmo.

The Mess Hall was hot and noisy. Ahead of them a dank-haired airman was arguing with a friend: Well he said That's what we're dying for isn't it? Grisby looked at Simon from cornered eyes and held up the while a finger to indicate one egg not two. A tall Negro with shades delicately ladled it out. Un oeuf Monsieur le Lieutenant? He nodded and said Like the French. Grisby queried. Simon said What it means is one egg: the French never eat more than one egg because one egg is *un oeuf*.

Grisby grimaced: you're adjusting too much to this place JP – turn into a Frog yourself in no time. Simon said it could be worse: Best cooks in the world these French.

Oh no sir said a voice behind them. It was an Airman Second Class he didn't know. Looked like Andy Hardy. Simon asked whose he liked better: German?

Oh no sir my mom's the best cook in the world.

The tall Negro dropped and broke the yolk of the fellow's egg. He was very black the server was and notoriously successful with the French girls. The lighter colored Negroes didn't do so well if they could be mistaken for Arabs.

The serving line moved on in front of the tall mural ordered by Colonel Mousse and painted by an airman he considered to have talent. On the wall was every aircraft that flew in WW2 from P40s to Messerschmitts to Zeroes to B17s to C45s all in one big dog fight/cargo carrying/bombing run combination. He and Grisby went to the Officers' portion of the hall and sat facing away from the mural.

As basic hunger was being assuaged he asked Grisby if by chance that was Jan (The Lovely) Gooley in his sack. Of course not he said: Does Cosmo ever eat here or only at the Club?

Club. Now who is she?

You know the reason I think I couldn't stand to eat at the Club isn't the cost it's Mrs Burger.

My God you had Mrs Burger in the sack!

No JP I remain one of the minority that has not tasted her favors. I would not in fact do her with your wee-wee. And you may as well stop asking: come over tonight after Bingo and I'll introduce you. Providing there's no gossip between now and then.

D'accord. Grisby looked at him menacingly. Agreed he said Agreed.

He tried to talk Grisby into skipping Bingo but he declined: Go to the flicks JP you'll like it. He asked what it was. A horse race thing: very exciting. Saw the Chaplain there having a fit.

Ratty?

No not the Catholic the other one. Laufer.

I'm surprised: would have thought he'd avoid that sort of thing. Since it involves gambling.

No said Grisby He was there.

They left but would meet for a PX break. They were supposed to say BX for Base Exchange but PX was somehow easier so they said it the way they did back in the Brown Shoe Air Force. The BX itself separated them from their offices: a low flat building like all the rest in the midst of a treeless lot. He often said some trees ought to be planted and Grisby as often thought it funny: they were not themselves going to be there that long before the French reclaimed it. He told Grisby the world was not a desert when they were born into it but Grisby only shrugged.

Simon went back to his BOQ room feeling good about having awakened that day to find himself irrevocably Intellectual. The way he supposed Homosexuals one day awoke to their condition: unfortunate but at least one knew one's name. Which of course was what Intellectuals did: they named things. Adam must have been the first Intellectual since to him was given the duty of naming all animals: what you can name you know and thus own. Which was why God hid His name from man and only comparatively late in human history did He reveal it: Rick.

Passing Shaw's door Simon saw the ready chess set and no Shaw: in the latrine maybe. Quickly he went in and playing white moved Pawn to Queen 4. Then he listened at Grisby's door but hearing nothing went on to work. The game had begun.

II

The First Sergeant was hiding his hangover behind the Paris edition of The New York Herald-Tribune but drawered the paper when he saw his Adjutant. The Morning Report Clerk and the Records Clerk were both working on the coffee pot and said they were moving it down to the Day Room. Cholmondelay who pronounced his name with four syllables not two was nowhere in sight. Where was he? The First Sergeant thought about it: Pioneering the thirty hour work week he said. Well find him and set him to work doing something: justice must not only be done it must seem to be done. Yes sir said the Sergeant who knew well how things ought to seem.

Simon picked out a manual at random but pretended it was by design and went to his office. There really was nothing to do between then and the time to sign the Morning Report but he had to seem busy. He would study for Matt Shaw's class. Tuesday and Thursday nights for eight weeks would get him three semester hours more. Already he had taken all the French grammar and lit courses they offered. He read **The Social Contract** till it was ten o'clock. Then he called Grisby and got ready for the PX run. He put the pocket book in the side drawer under the .45 kept there for wearing on days when the troops were paid. He locked the desk.

It was still a cool and high blue day that now suggested football more than Spring but that was how it was in Europe. Yurp as Jan called it. And there she was! With Nurse Forney who was not her roomie though oddly enough her sometimes pal: both were Irish Catholics but they shared nothing else. One was the Desired Product and the other the Failure or maybe she was the

Second-Best product: at least Forney was a Total Pagan and not a Protestant. He recalled what Scott Fitzgerald had said of his Catholic upbringing: that it had ruined him for Paganism. Not so for Forney.

Jan waved and smiled her big melon slice and turned back on her way while Forney never turned her face toward him at all only rolled her ripe posterior melons at him once or twice and resumed normal ambulation. Would Jan really prefer BM? No doubt Stocks-and-Bonds would sound like a better provider-to-be. Better than whatever he was going to be: an Intellectual. Which normally was thought of as contrary to Catholic: anti-Catholicism was the Intellectual's anti-Semitism. So long as Grisby didn't turn RC. So far as Jan was concerned Grisby's P and his own blank space amounted to the same thing and indeed the Air Force thought so too since when they asked P or C or J? he said *Nothing* and they started to put down P and it took quite a protest to keep it limited to Name Serial Number and Blood Type. There was no quarrel with B Positive.

His and Jan's only religious discussion had begun and ended at the Club shortly after they met when she said I bleeve what I bleeve and you bleeve what you bleeve. Then she added a Ha Ha to indicate no hard feelings. It was stalemated and would have so remained had not the Jewish Dr LtCol Burger in frustration grabbed their hands and forced them together: My God he said You two are young you're young! He would not let them separate their fingers and thus they sat till slowly they shyly knit together more agreeably on their own. Burger wasn't a bad fellow at all but oh my God his wife. BM especially disliked her.

In civilian life he and BM would not be friends but here their differences were suspended pro tempore. Grisby would know what sort of shirts to wear and ties appropriate to the shirts and with what coat and he had a role to play and so on. At the moment their shirts and ties were identical. Shaw had said a good anthropologist could still tell their Class Differences even so: by the way they talked or without hearing Talk he could tell by the way they walked or without seeing Walk merely by the way they stood. Simon would have to observe Grisby or rather Cosmo more closely. What would he be able to say about Jan?

At the PX Grisby was looking at a Grundig radio. They avoided the snack bar and the wet floor/hot air/quick food. I intend to buy one of these

JP said Grisby Just as soon as my ship comes in. Was it expected soon? Momentarily he said Momentarily. His face suggested that more would be heard of his plans anon.

I think I'd buy a Meerschaum pipe.

You ever smoke a Meerschaum pipe JP?

No but I will smoke a Meerschaum pipe if my ship comes in.

Negative thinking said Grisby quickly: *When* JP not *if.* He agreed: When.

They looked over shirts and insignia and household goods for the married and movie projectors and motor bikes and camel saddles and jackets. These last were of the silky kind best worn with well-greased hair and were hung with the backs showing a map of France with a star where La Beauce Air Base was and that was stitched on too and the dates 1953-56 or whatever years the tour had been. Cholmondelay who was the man Grisby said would some day rape their daughters had one. The camel saddles were for the air crews who flew toilet paper to Algeria and wanted them. The married would put one at your feet when they had you over for dinner while they got the projector out to show their home movies. There was no TV in the trailers so they bought Grundigs and cameras instead.

It was in someone or other's trailer that he had been paired at dinner with Jan Gooley. Immediately he sensed a chemical reaction but not hers for him: it was for Grisby who was seated next to a grade school teacher. Grisby seemed to sense that he was the cock of the walk. And seemed not to favor either woman. But Gooley liked Grisby. You ever date Jan he asked.

Once or twice said Grisby bent and fiddling with a Grundig. Then he stood: Makes you wish you were back in the Land of the Big PX eh JP? Back in the Land of the Round Door Knobs?

Actually I had forgotten for a minute that I wasn't back in America till you mentioned it Gris. There was a difference in that here he had more money to spend but he didn't say that. The goods were laid out row after row on linoleum tiled floors below fluorescent lighting. Grisby looked around at it all and prepared to leave. You know JP it's like the fellow said: all we'd have to do is bomb Moscow with Sears catalogs and the revolt would be on.

Naw Gris they'd never believe it: the Soviets would say it was all propaganda and the people would believe them. They'd have to believe them. He was looking at a sweater that was a copy of late 1930s style and was thus a twin of one he had been given at a Thanksgiving outing: It was our Johnny's old one that he left behind when he went away to the War and never came back the mother said And we'd like you to have some socks of his too. Sometimes where orphans were lent out for holidays they gave you new stuff and only claimed it was old but that one was old: a sleeveless sweater with zigzags on it. He had kept it ever since and wore it still in his BOQ room in cold weather.

His stomach sank. Because of the sweater? Or because Jan cared not for him? Or because of the Sears catalogs? As they passed the snack bar a song he'd never heard from a singer he didn't know came out: *Because I never thought / that I'd ever lose your love dear / you got me cryin the blues.* He would remember not to drop his g's. He left Grisby to go by Shaw's BOQ and sure enough the door was open and the Professor not there. But a piece had been moved: Shaw had shifted his Queen's Pawn to face his. He looked around and seeing no one moved his Knight to King's Bishop Three and left.

Fifteen minutes after he got back to his office the Morning Report was ready. He spent another fifteen minutes checking it before he signed and returned it. Then he went back again to **The Social Contract** until it was time for lunch. He went first to the BOQ. Grisby was waiting at the door to their latrine and after seeing he was alone asked him in to his room: There she is.

He stood back to allow himself full view of the bed: on it under a sheet except for the sticking-out feet and ankles was a supine female form. She seemed not to have moved since morning. It did not look like Jan Gooley. Her size. But wrong somehow. That was a relief. Then he realized why it was unlike her: the figure was not breathing. Is it a corpse Grisby? No he said Not at all and lifted the cover slowly and it was for the first time clear that the toes were not distinguished one from another but were only painted to show division and that the thighs were joined at the hip in sharp creases with the torso. The creases were neat and circular and there was no hair between: God covered His mistakes with hair. Architects used ivy and MDs used grass but God used hair. Except for a lengthwise female dimple there were no privates.

Grisby moved to the top of his bed and bent over and picked up the two corners of the sheet and indicated that Simon was to do the same. Together they folded it like a flag and with as much ceremony. Where did he get her?

From a shop in Paris. Had a damned hard time of it too JP because of my poor French but I was helped by my good money. And frankly I was uncertain whether to let you in on it back then (I've had her for a month) or I would have taken you along and let you handle French for me. I've just begun work on her he said and pointed to a small pin hole a slight bit north or where the proper orifice ought to be. Wasn't that a trifle small?

It's not the urethra JP it's where I've started to cut. The real thing will be back down an inch and a half or so from there but I had to wait till I got a bigger bit for my brace. He waved his hand at some tools in the top of his closet: That's where I keep her and you may notice there is a padlock on it to which I alone have a key.

Sort of a chastity lock?

Have to JP or the maids would find her. They've tried to get in even so. Grisby put his arms under her shoulders and made her sit up. Stiffly she showed her hard-looking face. It was painted in the then fashionable I've Just Come From Six Months in a TB Sanatorium look. She had an ashen complexion with pale lips and grey shadowing around the eyes with black liner. Large nippleless breasts: odd. The hair was painted on and was close to the skull. He raised an arm and on seeing no hair painted there assured Grisby she was not French.

I know: I plan to glue on two Brillo pads.

Really?

No. Take her feet and help me move her into her place in the closet. There were two hooks wrapped with wash rags to cradle her arm pits and there was another with a towel on it that fit under her fork. The head socked back into a sort of wishbone retainer on the wall.

You've gone to a lot of trouble Gris.

True. As soon as I can I figure on buying a carrying device. Probably a bass viol case.

You could get her one of those plastic bags they put air crewmen in when they crash.

Don't be crass about the woman I love. He picked up a rag and began thoughtful dusting. Got the idea for her one night when I was talking with Bowwow – engineer in aircraft maintenance. Tallish skinny fellow. Big mop of black hair. Most complete engineer I've ever seen – thinks if he farts that it's eighty percent methane and ought to be captured bottled and sold.

Simon knew him but under his born name and not Grisby's appellation.. And did Grisby's new love have a name?

Dunno. Thought maybe you could help on that. Something French. She look French to you?

Not much. Her form was designed for clothes horsing and was minimally feminine. Except for the large breasts without nipples. Otherwise boyish the way most fashion designers preferred. Real women wrongly thought that was what men preferred. He had seen a nippleless woman in Lorraine and thought Nancy might do for a name. But a name more Frenchy would be better.

We'll think of something Gris.

Lunch time JP. Let's take it at the Club. Phone in that you'll be a bit late getting back..

Cosmo was alone at a table and welcomed them. Just back from Germany he said and gave them a purposeful stare. Grisby spoke: Big things going on in Germany Cosmo?

Big said Cosmo darkly Very Big. He spoke as if his mouth were full of food or fitted with braces. Probably Cosmo had braces once. He wasn't sure if Grisby would have though he supposed so. Of course no orphan got braces and indeed one had to go up several social steps to locate folk who did. He thought he would like some day to have children so they could wear braces. As he was told that some folk had children so they could send them to private schools.

Grisby asked Cosmo if the doings in Germany were anything he cared to tell them about. Cosmo shook his head and then shook it again: You'll hear when and if the time comes Grisby (though if we're lucky and if things by some fluke work out then you won't hear).

It must be exciting being in Intelligence Simon said and Cosmo grunted agreement but Grisby looked as if nothing could possibly be more boring.

Fantastic said Cosmo Unbelievable. Better than flying he said. Cosmo wasn't rated: something about his ears. There was a snort from a near table from which someone was getting up and throwing down his napkin: a Lieutenant he didn't know.

What the hell is the purpose of the Air Force if not Flying? He was a dark fellow who was another blue jaw like Simon. He picked up his napkin again and wiped his mouth and threw it down again while looking at Cosmo and Grisby with disgust and at him for agreement since JP had wings. *D'accord* said Simon and the fellow swore competently in French and left.

Don't know him said Cosmo in a tone that meant the fellow didn't exist.

Name's Longbow said Grisby and spelled it: He's a pilot they brought in to play football.

Ah said Cosmo Then he does have a function after all: for the ancients the heavens hung low but now some of us can fly over Olympus and some who do so think they're gods. I'm mixing metaphors of course since low heavens for the ancients meant the gods were paying attention.

Only paranoids have that privilege now said Simon.

And people in Intelligence work said Grisby: They impose their own meaning. Or paranoia as JP says. For the Paranoid and the Elect everything makes sense.

We're playing for the Forces of Light against those of Darkness said Cosmo. It was his turn to put down his napkin: Got to leave now for he said and caught himself just before giving away Significant Information. For places best left undisclosed he said smiling upside down at his almost error and waved them goodbye.

He asked Grisby after Cosmo's real name and was told a very ordinary one. So it happened that Grisby was one who also could see through appearances to essences. Perhaps underneath it all Grisby was an Intellectual too: Grisby-the-name-giver. If he gets Cosmo then why only JP for me? Grisby shrugged and said that was what he was.

OK then for Bruce M Grisby it's BM.

Not if you want any of what's hanging in my closet. And of course if you breathe a word to any about her —

My lips are sealed Gris. And I've thought of a name. Grisby asked what but before he could answer Longbow came back followed by the wife of an MD: Mrs LtCol Burger herself. Simon had first met her months before in a Maryland lit class where she had got very excited over a new Irish writer James Jewess as she called him since she was from Philadelphia and had an unfortunate dialect. She was trim though and smoldering and had desperate eyes but she was wringing her hands. That was a bad sign. Longbow came back to his deserted table where the soiled dishes still lay and pulled a cigar from his pocket and lit it while she hurried into the chair opposite him: All I want to know she said Is Whoy! Whoy!

That's all you want from life said Longbow as he drew in his first puff: You don't want to do Something Big you just want to know Why?

She wrung her hands at him afresh by way of answer. She had to bring them up from her lap to do it.

I'm sorry he said that such is the case because I could answer the other: my daddy always told me that if you want to do Something Big you could maybe wash an elephant. Longbow avoided looking at her. But he never told me Why. She continued to wring at him although her hands were running down. Then her hands collapsed to the table cloth and she began to cry quietly and then to laugh loudly. She got up and pushed her chair in and turned from Longbow to the two of them: All I want to know is what it meeeans she said without really looking at them and went past them toward the back door. There they could see she had met Shaw. She was in his class too. She had his lapels and was demanding something from him. You think he'll be able to tell her Grisby asked. Simon shrugged. Longbow meanwhile had settled back with his cigar: a woman is only a woman. Simon decided Kipling was an Intellectual too.

What's the name you have picked out?

Huh?

Grisby repeated the question. Oh: Marianne he said and spelled it. She was the one who took off her shirt and led the charge at the barricades. In 1848 I think. Wore a floppy red hat and carried the flag.

No brassiere? I guess they didn't have them then?

That's how they paint her: both of em hanging right out. Nice too. Funny what different nations choose for their symbols. None of our people ever thought of Molly Pitcher that way.

Marianne isn't a bad name. Led a charge where? When? During one of the revolts? Grisby said he thought the revolution was in 1776. In fact there was an old farm house on the base with that date bricked high up into its main chimney. The authorities were tearing down the farm house. That chimney hadn't anything to do with us?

A coincidence Simon said. The French had their revolutions too. Lots of them. Some say they got the idea in part from us. I doubt it: just Intellectuals trying to assign a reason for what happened. It was the Middle Class who did it -- taxed too much to pay for French support for our rebellion: the Lower Orders will riot but they haven't the staying powers to keep at it. Louis in supporting us brought on his own demise. But the revolt came from the Middle. It always does. After the dust settled the Middle Class was in charge. Shaw says people seldom fight for Ideas: only Money. Or Power. Pretty much the same thing said Grisby. Simon said Intellectuals write the texts to say how ideas that preceded the acts caused the acts. But they're just giving themselves airs: no one besides intellectuals think intellectuals are important. One intellectual (a historian) early in 1789 proclaimed that revolution was imminent – church and state and aristocracy were rotten and collapse was imminent. If he hadn't been English and talking about England he'd be famous today.

Grisby said Simon had been in one class too many of Shaw's but he liked the name of Marianne. They got up to leave. Longbow was still quietly studying his cigar. A good cigar is a smoke he said.

At the back door Shaw was newly freed from Mrs Burger and was chuckling to himself. He recognized JP from his class and stopped him: Whatever do they want hey? As the beloved doctor of Wien asked Whatever do they want? Then he launched off to the bar. Shaw smelled strongly of herring and something else. He'd didn't know what.

Grisby said it was vodka. But that wasn't supposed to smell. I can smell it said Grisby: It's on his cat's breath too.

Outside the door sat the cat unsteadily waiting her master's return. She ignored them as they passed even when Grisby stepped on her tail. They turned and looked at her but except for a burp she made no acknowledgment.

Grisby stopped at his room and Simon went on past the cat's master's open door where he saw Professor Shaw had moved his Pawn to Queen Four which he balanced with his own Knight to King's Bishop Three. Outside the BOQ he saw three nurses he didn't know who were on their way to somewhere or other who were discussing another woman: And she sleeps with enlisted men one said But only with black ones. Another nurse said *Oh* and the third nodded that it was so. Then they passed on.

FOOLS AND DAMN FOOLS

It is not enough to say that the difference between the Fool and the Damn Fool is that the former asks what the difference is and the latter tries to answer: the difference more nearly parallels the distinction between the Merely Intelligent and the Intellectual. Be it understood first off that this distinction is not one discerned by differences in degree of intelligence since being Intellectual is more of a Cast than a Quality of Mind: by far most Intelligent people are not Intellectual and any number of Intellectuals are not very Intelligent.

The Intellectual is one who asks Why, and Socrates is the Western prototype thereof: when on trial for his life he was offered the chance to live if only he would shut up, but of course he said that the resulting life would not be worthwhile. The unexamined life is not worth living, he said. By which he implied that the examined one is.

The Intellectual is like Thoreau afraid that he may come to die and realize that he has never lived. (Thoreau was afraid to marry since it would mean a loss of Self: he thought of himself as a Self-Contained Unit.) The Intelligent fellow is not like that and does not worry that he may come to die and realize that he has never lived. He seldom thinks about that sort of thing at all. When he comes to die he still doesn't think about it.

The Intellectual on the other hand worries about it all the time. Then when he comes to die he realizes he has never lived (unless his Ideas have been Realized and people have been controlled by them). Although it is true that some Intellectuals have a handle on the amorphousness of what they deal with, see that tossing about globes of gelatine can be sloppy. Scientists are not Intellectuals, at least not when doing Science, and may the heavens help us when they try to do so in other fields. As Paul Valéry had it, "Il ne faut appeler Science que l'ensemble des recettes qui réussissent toujours. Tout le reste est littérature." Science is a list of recipes that always turn out and all the rest is Literature. And Literature in none of its offshoot branches is Science.

III

As soon as Simon was back in his office the First Sergeant came in and said Cholmondelay had been located: the Air Police had him on a charge of Public Brawling. He had got into some sort of fight with an Army man in Paris. The Provost Marshal would deliver him on demand. The First Sergeant was told 1400 would be fine and Simon got out the Uniform Code of Military Justice commonly called the Gospel According to Twining. An hour later the First Sergeant came in with a small dark rat with hope in his rodent eyes: hope that the Article 15 punishment he would be offered in lieu on a Summary Court Martial would be lenient. With a Summary he would surely go back to Airman Third but with a Lieutenant (young ones were easy) he could get maybe two weeks of restriction and keep his two stripes. He saluted sharply and in so doing showed a set of scraped knuckles. His nose had looked broken for as long as JP had known him but was freshly taped. The senior AP handed over the report.

The fight was over a whore that Cholmondelay regularly bought from in Pigalle but who had other allegiances also: an Army PFC from Orleans had challenged him on who had immediate priority. That basically was it. All those there but Cholmondelay were asked to leave and even the First Sergeant saluted sharply when they did so: encouragement to nail the little bastard. With them gone and Cholmondelay asked to choose a Summary or an Article 15 he took the latter. He was warned that anything said from then on could be used against him. Agreed.

All right Airman tell me in your own words what happened.

Cholmondelay's eyes grew slightly more slitted than their puffiness required and looked around for permission to sit. Getting none he drew up again and probably wondered if he'd been as well off with a Summary: probably not since it they went to all that trouble they expected you ought to pay.

Begin please.

Yes sir well there's this girl named Monique –

A whore.

Well yes sir I guess some people would call her that but I happen to think a lot of her sir and would just as soon not hear her talked about that way. He drew up to at least 5' 5".

Nonetheless that is how she makes her living? Yes sir. Then continue. Well sir I was just coming in and there was this Army guy there who didn't have any business there since he was already back on the street and then he just sort of sneaked back in and once he was there he wouldn't leave and so I was going to go on right there in front of him and she uh washed me off in the sink like they do you know before you start in on the real thing and this Army guy comes up and starts to piss in the godam sink and I was so f –

Watch your language.

Yes sir I got so mad I told him when he got through that in the Air Force they taught us to wash our hands after we got through pissing and he said in the Army they taught them not to piss on their hands. I mean urinate. And I couldn't let him get away with that about the Air Force and here I am.

And that's all?

Yes sir.

From the AP report that seemed to be generally true. OK: the basic problem here Cholmondelay is that you seem not to understand that you're not an ape you're not in the jungle anymore. (Was Cholmondelay Negro and likely to take an unintended offense? No. No offense. But maybe part Negro.) Not in the jungle anymore and frankly we can't have people behaving that way. It's not civilized. Now you notice we both are in uniform and of course that is civilized and such is the way people ought to fight if they have to fight at all: of course our role in the military is to prevent war by being prepared to wage one. Now obviously this does not mean that civilized man does not fight but it does mean that he fights in civilized ways over civilized matters: not over a paid woman in a cheap hotel off Pigalle. You understand?

Cholmondelay said he did. Obviously he didn't. What you have to understand Cholmondelay is that we fight people we don't know rather than people we do know: probably we can't even see them. This is especially true in the Air Force. (Or did you know him? You did?) Well to reiterate we fight not over some piece in a hotel room the way dogs and cats might but what we do if we're civilized is we fight unknown people over issues of great importance. In fact the issues are of such great and mysterious importance that very frequently we don't at the time even know what it is we are fighting for. Although at the time we're very certain of it. Probably the French thought their revolution of 1789 really was for Liberty Equality Fraternity but when the dust had settled in a generation or two those in control were the Bourgeoisie. So that's what you do: don't listen to the rallying cries of the moment but wait for a generation or two and see who's in control. That's how we learn what wars and revolutions really are about.

Cholmondelay stood looking at him. Cholmondelay had not been in two courses with Shaw.

He cleared his throat and pulled Cholmondelay's pass and then told him he was restricted to the base. He could go to the Mess Hall for meals and to Church on Sunday if he wished and besides that he was to be in the barracks. Also he would have KP. So Cholmondelay who was pleased at having got off lightly and having guessed right saluted and left. He had won but not for the reasons he had expected: the Noble Savage was corrupted by Civilization (though barely) and it was hardly the fault of the Savage.

The First Sergeant came in for a report and was disappointed but then was reassured when told responsibility for enforcing Cholmondelay's restriction was his: one false step and they'd bring him back in and take a stripe. The First Sergeant smiled saluted and left. He would enforce it indeed. Poor Cholmondelay. Poor JP: he wished he had a job like Cosmo's which was analogous to that of a bombardier looking at the landscape from 40,000 feet where it seemed a map with no people. He wished intensely that he were flying both for that reason of avoiding people directly and also because it offered more adventure than piloting an LMD: Large Metal Desk. Navigators also were morally neutral: he took them there and back but did not decide where they were to go or what was done when they got there. In that regard it was like Science or Math. He laced his hands in back of his neck and leaned back in the swivel chair closing his eyes after noticing that the entire Cholmondelay affair had required only fifteen minutes. The clock was about to make the quarter hour tick: it was shirring up for that and he could hear it.

Then as if he were looking through the old stereoscope some kids found in a desk drawer at the orphanage he saw himself: the pictures that went with the stereoscope were of Great War soldiers about to go over the top (many were dead moments after the photo was made but in the intense 3D of the stereoscope they would live forever) and of couples seated circa 1900 in plush chairs with ferns and gee-gaws about (they were 80 by then if still alive but young and proper and horny in the next room in the photos). The silence was terrible. Something was missing from those photos. Time. Time was what was missing. And then he was on the ceiling.

Even so and from that elevation did he suddenly see as if for the first time truly. He was himself the subject in two side-by-side photographs: there he sat arms locked behind his head but alongside that seated self was another scenario. In it he was standing with his .45 drawn and aiming and about to fire at someone. At Cholmondelay. Both scenes were a sort of Little Theatre production where he was miming his lines. The two scenes were side by side amidst haze yet he himself was not in either place: where he was it was Real but the scene at the desk was not and neither was the scene of him squeezing the trigger . He saw himself in both at once. And then he left that place on the ceiling where Reality was and again was at the desk acting a part.

The clock whirred and hit quarter-past.

He wrote down the experience to tell Shaw about and ask him what that sort of thing meant. Then he went back to reading **On the Origin of Inequality Among Men**. The book now seemed to be lacking in dimension. Previously it was OK. It was interesting thinking still but now was superficial. However he had it nearly finished by the time he met Grisby for the PX break and was well into **Thus Spoke Zarathustra** by quitting time.

Since Gris planned to go to Bingo anyway Gris said he would wait to eat late at the Club in fact would eat and play at once and planned to work till then (alone but thanks anyway) on (what was her name?) Marianne? So JP should go on without him. So he did.

The Club was styled in Wicked Howard Johnson's: spic and span and done up in red and black and quite dark at places and in particular at the bar although the dining area was bright enough. In the back was a closed off portion reserved for private parties and crap games and he never went there. Few persons were as yet feeding and there was no one he knew well enough to sit with so he took a two-place table out of the way. He passed a table of pubescent girls who were just finishing perhaps before going to the early movie: one of them was telling a dirty joke he'd already heard about a newly-wed Cockney wife arskin er usband Ow about gettin orf. He thought it was Colonel Mousse's daughter who was the raconteuse. Or Burger's. He sat out of ear-shot from them.

A German girl with a face like a peeled potato and who was an axe handle across the beam gave him a menu and waited. Most of the kitchen help even as the Band were usually from Germany. Also some of the civilian maintenance help. They were more used to American ways than were the French. And more amendable to getting used to them. The food wasn't bad: somewhere between Mid-German and Mid-Western American but he couldn't quite decide and the girl fidgeted twice and said she would be back shortly. A hand clapped him on the shoulder and then swept to the chair opposite which he pulled back for the body of uh Longbow the uh football player and sometimes pilot. Boy you look about as nervous as a queer eating a hot dog.

No not nervous just undecided.

Same thing said Longbow and waived the waitress back. Potato face brought him a menu of his own. She moved off again and they studied until a Lieutenant Colonel he immediately recognized said they looked like two book ends waiting for a library. A very clever comment for a Lieutenant Colonel. Don't you two know each other?

Sure we do said Longbow We just don't like each other. The LC laughed and went on.

Longbow said he was Doctor Burger the Unfortunate.

Unfortunate? Oh yeah: it's his wife who's always asking —

Always said Longbow: you ready to order? He was. They ordered as it happened identically. Both got German beer. You could get either American or German for a quarter. They looked after Burger's retreating back and shook their heads in unison.

A few older women were coming in even though it was a good hour and a half before Bingo. You a careerist Longbow asked. Yes: was he? Longbow nodded and said he hoped to retire with thirty years as at least an LC. They studied the several buxom waitresses: their make-up wasn't on right and their hair didn't suit but they were fast enough and the silverware came clean and hot from the kitchen and the table cloth smelled fresh and had no stains on it. He asked Longbow why he liked it enough for a career.

Because there's no damned sentiment about it: even the Chaplains have enough sense not to talk about Love. And it is Selfless: in War you can lose yourself. Longbow smiled. He liked War. Didn't Simon like War? What did he think they were in the Air Force for? Peace?

Well no he knew it was for war but he didn't think they were supposed to like it.

You sure you ain't no Chaplain? (Where was he from?) Luzana said Longbow: my name is French not Choctaw. It's a English corruption of a

French name: the Lamb. OK you want me to look into my heart? OK I do that: and what I find there is War. Peace said Longbow at his newly arrived pork cutlet Is abnormal: the normal estate of Man is War. And since I want to be in on that sort of thing I stay in. You been in the military in time of war?

Technically the Korean thing but really not much of it.

Longbow chewed on his food like a thoughtful dog. Looking around he said he'd seen this place before.

Oh do you have déjà-vu experiences too?

Longbow nodded and asked did he speak French. Yes but why do you ask?

Because you just spoke some.

Oh: I'm part French. I think. That so said Longbow. And you too asked Simon? Am I what? Was he all French? No he said I'm a Eskimo.

How strange said JP: I am part Eskimo too. I think. Longbow finished his beer and indicated to the waitress his desire for another one. She was prompt with Longbow and Simon was impressed since they usually ignored him.

You're not sure about much are you Simon? Don't know whether you're an Eskimo I mean.

He explained that he was an orphan.

The news was acknowledged. Well he said I've made a few of those but I'm not one myself. While the waitress poured his new beer he said he had that déjà-vu experience himself. The girl thought he was talking to her and tried to look amused. Gradually she saw the truth and went off. I don't like them Longbow said Because they're like pieces from a puzzle that you don't have the picture of to copy and they appear suddenly when you're not ready for it and then just as suddenly they gone and you realize that even though it's a very important puzzle there are at least 1000 pieces to it and anyway you just lost the one piece you did have and you only had it for a minute. Then you forget it until it happens again sometime when you're not looking for it and you're convinced that nothing else in life matters except solving that damn puzzle but at the same time you know there ain't no way you can solve it at least not on your own: it has to be given to you but there ain't any way you can ask for it or any way you can get it. It just comes and goes and leaves you confused. Why? You did just have one you say?

Yes. But JP preferred them to nothing. They also left him feeling that there *was* a puzzle. He decided not to tell Longbow about being on the ceiling that afternoon.

At the far end a space had been cleared in which was a roped-off table on which were flung assorted Bingo cards. The women and an occasional man were circling that. The rope was to protect the cards. The women who played a lot knew some cards were better than others and they thought they knew which ones. The rope was kept up till the whistle blew and then God help you if you were in between the table and the women at that point. He saw Mrs Burger down there among them with Lieutenant Colonel Burger not far off. Longbow was watching the two of them. And then he was up and fumbling for some scrip to pay his share: See you later Simon he said pronouncing the surname the French way and just as the whistle blew and the ropes were removed and the scramble began for the cards up front Longbow was gone out the back door.

At the bar it was quieter. And would remain so even after the game began except when O-69 was called and all the bachelors would raise their glasses and cheer. Without turning from the bar. Mainly family types had taken over the dining area and half of them weren't there primarily for the eating. There were few uniforms. He ordered a King Alfonso at the suggestion of the Sergeant from Base Supply who was picking up a few bucks tending bar. Not only did it taste good it was pretty: cream on top neatly divided from the dark liqueur on the bottom. Until you tipped it and let some slide back in and then it mixed in interesting patterns. He didn't know which he preferred: neat and contrasting or moiling and shifting as milk and alcohol resisted each other. As he studied he became aware of peculiar behavior on the part of the officers to either side of him and by the bartender Sergeant too: they were all looking somewhere else. It was because someone was standing behind him. The someone was not a tall man but was breathing down his neck. Not a man at all since there was perfume. He half turned and met the dark brown irises of Mrs Burger looking very liquid and as usual desperate as they fought off the surrounding whites: life for her was two Alfonsos always about to spill.

Well she said I suppose you don't intend to answer me. She stood under one of the lights hidden in the checkered ceiling and was flooded by it: a soft white apparition in a clingy red dress. What was that stuff called that her dress was made of it. It covered her chest but showed it too. Jersey.

The other Lieutenants were still turned half away. Answer you what? Maybe he said If you told me the question I could tell you the answer.

Her eyes clarified sharply and she drew in her breath so swiftly that her nostrils flared. She had no hair in them and he wondered how women did that: did they cut them out or did hair just not grow there?

Then she sighed: Yes I suppose you have phrased it well: Unless one knows the question there is no point in seeking the answer. So many never realize that there is a question so how could they possibly be aware that there is an answer? She waved her hands at the turned backs before her and included in her sweep all those now getting ready for the numbers to be called. Already they were tumbling in a rotary bird cage and another Sergeant picking up a few bucks or for something to do was about to announce the first call.

You know she said That is what I like about you: at least you are aware that there *is* a question. The fact is that most others either pretend there isn't one or else they really don't *know* there is one. As for the question it remains the same: What does it mean? Ah he said But our friend Bowwow the Engineer says there are No Valid Questions Without Answers: if there is no Solution there is no Problem sez he. Problems he says belong to Math and the Sciences. And not to the Inexact Sciences. She listened but deigned not to give the engineer's opinion so much as a shrug. She turned and moved away on nicely firm hams. As she moved out of the red lighting he saw her dress wasn't red at all but tan. Jersey was what it was. Also she had two pones that rode her thighs like jodhpurs. That was nice too: feminine.

He turned back to the bar and his drink. It was an even light brown color then and the struggle had finished.

A Defense Mechanism said the fellow at his right elbow now that he was willing to be acknowledged. It was Jake Segal. Fearless Jake. He flew too eagerly for a C119 pilot. The C119 was known to be a very forgiving aircraft but Jake was said to push it a bit. He had mentioned at another time that he was a trifle bored with flying toilet paper to the troops in Algeria.

What's a Defense Mechanism? Jake told him. OK he said But what's the Defense? Her asking that question? Nope said Jake And it's not our refusing to ask it: she justifies everything else she does by going around pretending to Ask Serious Questions – she'd run like hell if she got an Answer. Then Segal took a swallow and hurried it down to yell Yaaaay. The Sergeant who was calling the numbers had just said O-69.

As he left to go to the movie he met Grisby at the table selecting his card and grumbling that the good ones were all gone. He would see him afterwards Grisby would? Sure.

EPIPHANY NUMERO UNO

Architects cover their mistakes with ivy,
MDs with grass,
God with hair.

IV

It was to be a movie about horse racing but there was nothing else especial to do and somehow it seemed delicious to waste time so thoroughly as that so he got in line. It wasn't a long one and he was only fifteen or so from the ticket office when someone broke in directly behind whoever was buying his just then. It was a stocky man who from a distance looked short till you got close and then he towered: it was Colonel Mousse. Called Bull. The line grew suddenly silent and when the Colonel turned before going in and waved genially at them all. There was no response. Mousse seemed not to notice or else not to care and went on in. He made a thing of placing the fork of his trousers to the left of his genitalia: military men always Dress Right said Mousse. Then the silence slowly turned into grumbling. He paid his quarter when the time came and gave the ticket bought a bag of popcorn and found a place. There wasn't anyone there he knew. Yes there was: Laufer sat like the perfect stolid German bourgeois waiting for the entertainment. The Chaplain was the only officer he knew who deliberately got haircuts with sidewalls. And this on a head that looked like a peeled potato anyway. He went over and sat next to him.

Haven't seen this one eh Chaplain? As he spoke there came a grind and a click over the loudspeaker and then a whir and someone began singing about a Green Door. He liked that one. Laufer said Oh yes he'd seen it twice before: at both showings the night previous and he would indeed see it twice again that night. He would stay for the second showing. And perhaps he would come tomorrow night too. Oh: something here you can use in a sermon perhaps? Something scriptural?

No said the Chaplain with both hands on his knees Oh no: just entertainment. His knees and indeed his entire legs strained at the material. The hands were broad and flat and the fingers thick. But how could he enjoy it if he knew how it was going to come out?

Laufer was delighted to be asked: he glowed. It is like God he said For I know exactly how it is all going to happen before it happens (although that is not altogether the correct way to phrase it since for the deity it is always Now and there is neither before nor after). I find this very satisfactory. Exciting in fact.

Yes I suppose it would be. He decided to tell him about the episode on the ceiling and the two poses he saw there. The Chaplain nodded: Time he said Exists in order to keep everything from happening at once.

Someone began to sing about Cryin the Blues cause he never thought that he'd ever lose her love dearrr she'd got him crying the blues. The song was cut off half way through when the lights dimmed. The theater was almost filled. The week before they'd had **The King and I** and the troops who weren't used to a musical where people suddenly started singing in the midst of a conversation began stomping their feet and the showing had to be stopped twice in order to quiet them down. A horse race film would do them almost as well as a Lash LaRue.

Since Simon never cared who won the real thing it didn't matter who took the fictional one.

Except it made a difference in this case since if Old Hoof-Hearted lost then his psyche would be destroyed: he didn't know who the actor was but he had great faith in the horse (finally justified) and his girl friend was delighted too. Throughout it all the Chaplain smiled and from time to time nodded approval: yes it was going well going well. Laufer would not accept an offer to go to the Club after it was over but would indeed remain for the second show. So they parted.

At the bar there were few left not even Segal. He was a funny fellow but a madman: one day he promised he would bring in his C119 low over the apron when they were having a parade and he would do it upside down. But he was gone for the night the barman thought. He drank a bottle of Beck's and saw at the other end a woman he didn't know who was sitting more or less between two stools and drinking from a carafe of purple wine.

Who's she? Sergeant Leigh said he didn't know for sure but he thought she was named Compton and was the new librarian: Been in here every night drunk for a week. Now and then Colonel Mousse takes her home but not tonight. As he said that the woman shifted a buttock off one stool but failed to perch one on the lateral stool in time to prevent her sitting finally in between them. Numbers were still being called around the band stand and no one there seemed to notice. When it became clear that either she didn't intend to get up or else couldn't do so he went over and introduced himself and asked could he see here home. He could she said if he would be so kind. Her accent was thickly Southern but not quite like Longbow's. More genteel.

They went out the front door with her bumping loosely against him while he girded her with one arm and drank from his glass with the other. She slopped her wine about in the carafe at her side. As they left Colonel Mousse was coming in also probably from the movie (been held back to discuss the plot?) and the Colonel smiled broadly and held the door.

Half way to the parking lot her knees gave out completely and gently he let her down. He stood enjoying the quiet and the dark and starry night and slowly finished his beer. When done he stuffed the glass in a side pocket and arranged her carafe where he could pick it up once he got her in his arms.

She was totally dead weight and several times he thought of dropping the wine but didn't. Damnably she lived not only in a far BOQ with most of the other women (teachers nurses Special Services and an occasional WAF officer) but she was on the second floor. She wasn't out she was just limp and was able to direct him. Her door wasn't locked.

Once she was on her bed she looked rather peaceful: like a new corpse. Middle aged. Sleek and Chinesey like quite a few Mississippians. He took off her shoes and she smiled at the release. Then she said she had to get up for a minute. He leaned forward to help but she didn't need it. Wait here now she said and toddled into the latrine and turned on the water. She was gone two minutes and when she came back looked fresher but older. Her almond eyes were red for one thing. She tried to close the latrine door behind her but failed and then suddenly again unsteady lurched over and locked the front door and then collapsed again on the bed. Once again she looked peaceful.

A hand nervously searched at her left side meaninglessly until he realized what it was for. You've got your skirt turned around he said It's on the other side. She nodded with her eyes shut and told him to turn out the light. He left one on in the latrine. He opened and helped her out of her garments. She was no more hirsute than a twelve year old and looked to be gently holding a fortune cookie beneath and between her slender hips. Otherwise she was like a warm bed but she went to sleep too soon and became undesirable. She seemed content to have got her card punched and not to notice his going.

When he escaped to his own BOQ it was reasonably quiet except for Segal practicing the tuba. He was trying a Beethoven sonata for clarinet and wasn't doing badly. Certainly it was better than Boola Boola. He always finished with Boola Boola sometimes after playing Fair Harvard backwards. Segal was a Yalie.

Curiously the door opposite Segal's was open even though Hoop hated the tuba. Segal kept his closed but that wasn't enough. He looked into the well-lighted and tidy but vacant place that was Hoop's room. There was the framed photograph of Jesus all right but no Hoop. Then he heard him next door talking to Laufer with their voices carrying through their adjoining latrine. A Spartan place lacking in all decoration save the one picture. In the open closet hung the fringed leather jacket Hoop wore for dress-up. He went down the hall to Shaw's room and saw through the open door that the Professor had moved a Pawn to King Three. He countered a Pawn to Bishop's Four and left just as the toiled flushed. He went back to wait for Grisby.

Grisby wasn't there but showed up shortly smoking a long cigar and carrying a big stuffed black and white panda he'd won at Bingo. It had a small red felt tongue that stuck out. Grisby set it on a chair and after locking doors they got ready to bring Marianne out. What's his name Gris? Grisby didn't have one for it yet but pretended he did: Teddy he said.

Very clever: say did you know we could fix Teddy up the uh way we're uh doing Marianne you know? Uh you know maybe a prosthetic device?

You're perverted Simon you know that? Perverted.

Because Teddy's a male? Teddy doesn't look obviously male to me Gris.

Because he's obviously a bear: come and help me lift her down.

Chacun à son goût: you don't tell on me I don't tell on you. Then he got one arm and helped hoist her off the hooks. She's like a corpse Gris.

That'll be OK once you paint her face: won't look so dead when you get through. Go get your paints and work on the top side while I do that bottom. Make her look like something besides a frog.

So he did. With her legs shot straight up behind him he sat on the side of her bed and began to re-do her complexion. He changed her to a facsimile of the woman who haunted his dreams so that from the ashen she went to a pleasant pink. Grisby was boring away the while but complexion altering wasn't fine work and there was no problem. Would she have a wig? Oh yeah sure. Then get a red one he said: I plan on giving her green eyes and chestnut eyebrows. Grisby said OK and for him to buy it and he would repay him.

I'll look pretty silly buying a redheaded wig designed for a female.

No sillier than I would said Grisby And besides you're the one that's matching it up with her complexion. Then too: do you want shares or no?

OK: next time I'm in Paris. Which probably will be this week.

Grisby grunted and then puffed on his cigar. He studied her fork up close then stepped back to change his bit. He rested the cigar on the dimple and fitted in the biggest bit he had and guessed it at two inches in diameter. He had put a smaller one farther back.. Grisby fitted the bit in and bored again and then just caught the cigar before it would have rolled off and onto his bed. You know he said as he went intensely about his work If I had it to do over JP I think I'd be a doctor.

Well the pay's good. It isn't too late is it? What would it take? One year of sciences as an undergrad? Then four more. Very bad hours though.

Naw I guess not. But Burger says it's sure fire. Says 75% of every doctor's time is spent with women. His bit broke out the last piece of plaster and the plaster and the brace poked forward into the vacancy. Penetration however slight is sufficient to complete this charge he quoted from the UCMJ but Grisby only grunted. He began to file at the edges to soften them. Then he asked if Simon wasn't he going to paint some more.

Have to let it dry. Although I guess I could do the lips. He squeezed out some carmine and mixed it. With a slight flip or two he was able to make a cupid's bow.

Is that the way her mouth is supposed to be? Is that how it's molded?

No: but women make minor changes with lipstick. Haven't you noticed?

Grisby had not noticed. With his own immediate work done for the moment he watched the lips being reddened. Looks more American that way JP: good job.

Maybe. Only whores wore lipstick like that in France but he didn't see any sense in bringing that up just then. Would her mouth open? Grisby said he supposed that could be done but then she would look like a ventriloquist's dummy. And he wasn't interested in conversation.

Her jaw is set JP.

OK: how about the creases where the legs and arms joined?

Nothing's perfect.

He mixed in some yellow with the red and then a touch of brown to get the rich tone he wanted for eyebrows. He made them thick but well up from the eyes and rising curiously as if the girl were going to say O Reeley? Then it came to him who it was he was making her look like and who it was said O Reeley but he decided not to tell Grisby. Touching a bit of the red in with the skin color he made a tone suitable for nostrils and then he shaded her cheeks a little and put some above the eyes. He painted just a light border around the eyes and then said he'd better get some eyelashes too while he was buying the wig: hair had to be three dimensional. Then he whitened the eyeballs till they look mad and then added a clear green iris. You did want her eyes open didn't you Gris?

Sure he said Sure. Grisby was standing wide-legged before her still upraised lower limbs and appeared not to notice smoke rising in a delicate grey scarf from her crotch. Then Grisby saw him staring and suddenly he jerked her upright. My cigar he said I stuck it up her ass. They got her up and shook this way and that until finally it stopped rolling about inside and stuck out a half inch. It was not the hot end so Grisby was able to get hold and pulled it free and took it in to the toilet and flushed. When he came back Marianne was seated on the bed with her legs sticking straight out before her.

Come to think of it Grisby perhaps you'd like proctology?

He was ignored. Silence. The travel posters around the walls looked embarrassed. Well Grisby?

Damnit it JP I suppose you know you've made her look like Jan Gooley?

Oh. Did I? Hum. Well. Well we could rename her.

Grisby sighed: Let's put her up. Enough for one night.

OK he said But I have a couple of questions: for one thing those edges around the orifice are still pretty sharp and anyway there's nothing inside and for another those breasts not only lack nipples they're totally hard and for another the legs hardly flex at the hip. Grisby had gone to the refrigerator and drawn them out two Löwenbräu which he was even then uncapping. When finished with that he gave over the one then seated himself and sipping said he had those problems pretty well licked pretty well licked. Simon sat on a hassock and waited.

Well I had thought of giving her a mastectomy and then rigging up some supporting straps to hold a couple of bean bags filled with fine grain sand and putting a couple of falsies in them in front of the sand and that ought to be authentic enough. With baby bottle nipples. But I ditched it: too much trouble.

He took a swig: As for the legs I planned on sawing them off and then hinging them and putting the whole thing under a body stocking you know to make it softer. But it's too much trouble. All cats are gray in the dark.

Ben Franklin?

He nodded: When you go to buy the wig be sure to carry your easel: no one will give it a second thought. Most of his beer was gone and he studied the bottom of the bottle before continuing. As for the orifice I'd like the sort of prosthetic device that I've heard that queers use but I don't know where to get one if indeed there is such to be had. They make them for both men and for women don't they? I'd have the one that's a fake woman. It would be a witch to mount so I'll make do with my own fabrication.

He showed off the gizmo: it seemed to be an angora sock in a coil wrapped sleeve. Bowwow designed it for me he said.

Send it over to Base Maintenance for installing. Bowwow would see it as a challenge.

Thanks no. Cleaning it's going to be a mess. I suppose I'll just get a supply of socks. Soft ones. Anyway I've decided not to saw off those nippleless wonders. I don't want her to be a patchwork like something by Dr. Frankenstein. I already bought some falsies though. Know anyone who can use them?

I think I know where I can get rid of them. Grisby didn't ask him where but just gave them to him and said fine.

But first I would like to know why you're doing it: you know Gris that half the nurses are available and most of the teachers and if you don't want to get involved there are first class whores for trois mille. I do concede ten bucks is ten bucks but this seems to me a pale copy. As he spoke he considered Marianne again and saw little there erotic: two smooth bald globes on her chest and bald on top too and three holes below (one tiny one big one medium). Yet she smiled deliciously and her face though glazed was lovely. He thought of Jan and ached. The rest of her not so good. If they had proceeded with the cutting he would have renamed her Agatha for how she looked after the Romans martyred her. He said so.

Don't know much about that stuff JP but I do know that ten bucks is too much to blow that way with any regularity. I'm a follower of Saint Ben: he advised young men to take old mistresses so they wouldn't be pressured into marrying young. It's what he did in fact. Ben specified an old one because she wouldn't get pregnant or expect marriage and she'd keep it quiet and also be very grateful.

Simon said that was all true of Marianne except for the last.

Grisby shrugged: As Ben said all cats are grey in the dark. So is Marianne. Or so will she be. When we get through with her. That way I can build up my capital. He's the Patron of all Businessmen. A great man.

I thought it was Adam Smith. But wouldn't there be a bond formed even with a grey cat?

Grisby shrugged. He was asked if he wanted help putting her back up. Grisby looked troubled and at the moment it popped to Simon that it was that very morning that he had seen Marianne in bed with Grisby. So. Well perhaps in the morning then we'll put her up before breakfast. Grisby agreed to that.

In the hall it was quiet and ominous like a Van Gogh. Or maybe De Chirico. Except the shadows did not contradict: the walls were white and the floor checkered in large green and black squares under a pale yellow ceiling that was too well lighted. Only Hoop's door was wide open. Until he got right up to it he could hear only Segal's dying note of Dravrah Riaf. In a minute all hell would break loose but there would be some silence first while he cleared the instrument and got his wind back. Then Laufer's and Hoop's voices came through. They were talking about the movie and the significance thereof. It was easy to place the falsies gently on the bottom of the waste can beneath the desk.

Then when he raised his head there was the Sallman Christ looking off in genteel disapproval of all things gross. He took the picture and slid out the back. Then the print came out. With a pen from Hoop's own desk he signed it Yours Faithfully Jesus H Christ and put it back under the glass and then slid the cardboard support behind it. He left it as before on the desk and quietly retraced his steps down the hall and got to his door just as Boola Boola thundered out. As he was locking his door from within he heard Shaw singing an obscene drunken accompaniment.

V

There was nothing else to do on alternate Saturday mornings but pay the troops so once he got through with that he could leave for Paris. Actually there was nothing to do on the other Saturday mornings either but still everyone had to be there. Perhaps to keep them on the base and out of trouble one night more. He unlocked his desk and reached under his copy of **On the Origin of Inequality Among Men** for the .45 and found it and a clip and loaded it. The cartridge belt and holster were in a side drawer and with these found and put on he was ready to go for the money. That supposedly was the rule: if you were robbed while wearing a loaded weapon you didn't have to pay it back whereas if you were robbed when obviously in no way prepared to offer defense then you were liable. He felt very military with the .45 on his hip.

Grisby was at his desk doling out money to the various adjutants who came to sign for and collect the amounts. Also he picked up and signed for a bundle of French francs to be exchanged for dollars at the official rate of 350:1. None in his right mind ought to have bought them at that price since American Express gave you 400:1 and there were places where at little risk you could get 450:1. Even so most enlisted bought theirs at the official rate. There was time to speak to Grisby only long enough to inquire about their friend's health: was she on the mend? She was said Grisby who asked whether he planned a trip to Pairs as Cholmondelay called it and Simon said he was. He expected to take in an opera and he was indeed going.

Then don't forget to make your purchases. He said OK he wouldn't.

Grisby had promised often to go with him some time and take pictures. Simon did not look forward to that. He went back with his money and set up two small cardboard boxes for the charities of the day into which the foolish would throw some scrip from their miserable pay. Some of the older Sergeants did too. They seemed to think he cared and that it would help them in his eyes. As if he had any power that could do them any good. But perhaps you can't be too careful. They hardly knew the world of the officer and to them it may have looked mysterious. And you can't be too careful. Give some and maybe the Powerful will notice: but he didn't care. They lined up and saluted one by one and gave their name rank and serial number and were gone. Even so with Cholmondelay who was looking a bit better: the puffiness from the last Paris fist fight over a whore was receding.

The senior Sergeants were milling about waiting for him to leave so they could begin their poker or crap game. He'd never done that as an EM: too cautious. He returned the money to the Senior Finance Officer who was helping Grisby with the chore and again he told Gris he would remember. Grisby as a BBA was working at a semblance of his civilian career and hardly looked up. Grisby was happy.

At the BOQ he found the door open from the latrine to Grisby's room and checked in on Marianne. Painted she looked almost human as she hung there staring at him. He had done a good job on the eyes and they followed him but she badly needed hairs around them and on her head. And of course there were the two silly globes on her chest. Even so as he stared at her he ached for Jan.

Gris no doubt had left his closet open since there was no maid service on Saturday. Still it was careless of him. He locked his own latrine door after finishing a second shave and changing into quiet civilians: without yellow shoes or a camera there was no way to tell he was American. He picked up his paint bag and put in a change of socks underwear and shirt and compacted the easel for carrying and left.

Most officers and some enlisted men drove their own cars but he took the bus to the nearest town where the train stopped. One airman of Levantine extraction had bought an old but large limousine and spent his week-ends driving troops in and out of Paris for hire: they spent their francs on the whores but the Levantine did not. Smart. That was his name: Smart.

There were six to the train compartment none of them American and he began to feel free. Getting to the PX from the Gare took an hour via metro and bus which wasn't too bad: sweat and garlic and a certain perfume he knew not the name of seemed to predominate but these were agreeable. He asked a girl and she seemed not to mind: Ma Griffe she said. Once inside the PX it was if he had never left home: neon and linoleum.

But they had everything. Everything. Even eyelashes which came in several sizes and colors and the cheapest wig was expensive but he got an even more costly one since the cheapest looked like hell. It was Gris's money anyway. The clerks seemed to assume they were for Madame and there was no embarrassment. It was fitted into a plain bag and he got to his usual hotel in half an hour from the PX.

The concierge at the hotel near l'Etoile was happy enough to see him and pushed forward the usual forms to be filled out for the police. Happy in his job and why not? Like Grisby who had never gone through a stage of copying manuals and throwing away the copy work. There was some confusion about the room though: there seemed to be two rooms with the approximate same number and it was on the second try that he found the right one. One room and a bath complete. He buffed his shoes then left his rain coat behind and the easel and went out toward the Champs. Opera or a good meal? Couldn't do both since the opera was at eight and dinner in Paris didn't happen before seven at the earliest. It was a calm night. Perfect.

He passed a busy bar that was said by Cosmo to be frequented by chaps in Intelligence. Yes indeed that was just what Cosmo called it A Bar Frequented by Chaps in Intelligence. And by George there was old Cosmo at the bar about three people down. He started in and then thought better of it just as Cosmo turned and caught the corner of his eye. As he ducked out he saw Cosmo hunch forward as if not to be seen. He crossed the street and looked back to see Cosmo come out the doorway and then after locating him pretend to be elsewhere concerned. Simon went on in a hurry and took a seat at the second sidewalk café he came to and ordered a Martini: a cube of ice and a dash of soda and a twist of lemon he would like added to the sweet vermouth yes. The waiter acknowledged this and left. He lit his George Washington/Voltaire pipe.

At the first café to the right (the one he had just passed) Cosmo was lowering his long frame into place and ordering quite authoritatively if covertly. He looked like an SS member left behind except he was of course too young to have been commissioned over a decade although he looked similarly humane. When Cosmo saw him looking he put a copy of **The Times** in front of his face. Simon hailed a girl nasally singing out **New York Herald-Tribune** and got a copy from her. Now they were both hidden. His martini arrived and as he picked it up again there came on him the sense of déjà vu: Cosmo sitting there watching and himself sitting there pretending to be concerned and soon a girl in a pink skirt would come by and sure enough there she was.

Then it left as suddenly as it came and with the usual shudder. Unreal. Something was real but it was not what he was accustomed to seeing. He was a minor actor in a bad play.

He sighed and sipped. He did not hurry with the paper since it was his ball to run with or not: Cosmo was the one who had to watch and be apprehensive. Presently though he called for his bill and was given it and saw Cosmo do the same. Cosmo then paid but he didn't pay his own but only left it lying there and sat back: once you had ordered a drink the table was yours for so long as you wished as Cosmo well knew but as soon as you had paid your bill of course it looked as if you meant to go. So he waited and actually read some of the **Tribune**. It wasn't a bad paper: Liberal Republican in outlook. That was their game. Do good and get rich. Same as Liberal Democrats. Different ideas as to what doing good amounted to though. Cosmo followed him in due season to a book store farther down the street and browsed while Simon bought a copy of **The Outsider**. And a map of the city which though arty was accurate.

Cosmo was in the pornography section looking over something by Henry Miller. This was silly: Cosmo had no right to be spying thus since he was a head taller than any Frenchman in there and anyone asked half an hour later whether he had seen anyone unusual in the shop quickly would have described him. Possibly Cosmo's job wasn't so exciting as all that and he too pretended.

Next they went to the American embassy where Cosmo came after him into a men's room but not before Simon had time to get in a far stall and re-close the door and put his feet up against it so they couldn't be seen from underneath. The outer door opened and closed again and footsteps came slowly then quickly and then out again. He kept his feet up and read the first chapter. By then Cosmo was gone. Or did he only seem to be? No matter. The game was over since it took two to play and he had quit. Dinner was the ordinary tasteless American sort but was more or less digestible. American food sometimes gave him cramps but the meal was quick anyway and would allow time for the opera. He did not know which one it was but since he had seen three in his life likely it would be new to him. Though it wasn't too far to walk he took the Metro because he liked it and also did not want to be late. It was **La Traviata**. Good: that was not one of the three.

He bought the ticket behind a sort of female Cosmo who asked for *une billet* and who got told by the seller it was *un*. When his turn came he was careful to use the masculine article and the seller declaimed to him about how ignorant foreigners were. She spoke quickly and expected him to comprehend it all. He smiled nodded and moved on to make room. When he got to his box he saw that Cosmo was seated in the box to the rear of him. When he turned suddenly back to the front two of the people in his box noticed and so did one of those in Cosmo's box. Cosmo was outwardly unmoved.

Simon put his hand inside his coat and then withdrew it. Then he sat back to enjoy the show. Those around him were nervous. But their lives were more full. Probably he ought to leave at the end of act one or at the latest act two but he wanted to see if it came out happily. Cosmo was not in his seat at the start of act three and the people in his box were watching Simon. Then he saw Cosmo in the next box to his right. But he left before the end and didn't return: no doubt he knew the outcome of the opera. It ended sweetly indeed and Simon was quite happy with it. Cosmo and the female like him were not to be seen. Perhaps they had met and gone their way.

He went to **Le Trou Dans le Mur** and sat at the bar and had a couple of Tuborg beers and a hardboiled egg. It seemed an ideal bar and one that like the Opera and les Halles and the sidewalk pissoirs would be there forever. But it was best not to be alone in the bar and he was alone so he left. La Madeleine was not far off and on the streets nearby were the usual assortment of girls: high quality and somewhat expensive and as good as you could get on the streets. They never approached or even looked at potentials but were ready if approached. He approached one and was told trois mille and went with her. She was the sort officers bought from though it was odd that it should make any difference since the work they did was performed without distinguishing attire. Thought their attire and demeanor on the streets set them off from their Pigalle equivalents.

Shaw had said how ranks could be told apart even if American and in civvies: by the way they stood the way they walked the way their hair was cut the looks on their faces. All of that. Women too with their make-up and hair and fabrics. It came down to taste. Which was why one didn't buy at Pigalle. And why Cosmo looked different from him even in uniform.

She was lithe and clean and touching her was excellent so he tried to put off the conclusion of the affair. In time she grew tired of that although agreeable enough at first. When she began to press for completion he couldn't. You too drank she said and started to disengage herself but he wouldn't allow it. After more minutes and more protests from her the warmth wasn't worth the bickering and he relaxed his grip and she got off. Divorces probably happened that way: he would not rush into marriage. She replaced her brassiere and dress and shoes and politely left.

Back on the street he wandered a while and took a less than direct route back to l'Etoile. On a few walls anti-Algerian slogans appeared and now and then there was a circle with cross hair lines of a gunsight through it: Jeune Nation. In chalk. Why Young Nation? And older fading ones: Libertéz les Rosenbergs. Probably they had anti-Nazi stuff late in WW2 following pro-Nazi stuff earlier. Or else the reverse since the French were contrary. All that was gone anyway. He was glad that American politics were simpler and more sanitized. A bas avec les Juïfs. As he got closer to the hotel the scribbles got fewer. A bas avec Tout le monde.

At the hotel he again had trouble finding his room because of confusion about the door keys but on the second try found the right place: the halls on each floor were labyrinthine and certain numbers oddly repeated themselves but finally he found his place. There was nothing to do but go to bed. After washing he sat up for a while with his new book but had trouble getting a handle on it. So he turned out the lights. He opened the window and found himself over a courtyard. One could always jump and that would be the end of all his troubles. No it might hurt. And not be fatal. A mess for others. That was not the problem anyway (that there was no solution) since he was sure there was one but only had he not yet found the formula. One ought to be an Intellectual for at least a week before killing oneself. So he went back to bed and very soon slept.

Then the phone rang. He could not think what it was that was making the noise and then he cleared enough to know that it was the phone but hadn't before noticed he'd had one and it took time to find it. The voice spoke American and said I'm coming up OK? He mumbled and she asked again Is it all right? Sure he said and turned the key in the lock and switched off the light and got back in the bed. He fixed the covers so his head was mainly hidden but he could see out. Assuming she came from the lobby she found it with amazing speed but of course that was just it: she was looking for the other number and got his instead. Some fellow down the hall was lucky or soon would be. She was tall and blonde.

It's time she said setting down her things and then locking the door behind her. I've been thinking on what we said this afternoon and now is the time. I'm sure of it she said. Do you mind awfully if I spend the night here? Please don't say no it's taken me all evening to get my courage up and I couldn't think of anything else at the opera or eating since. I hardly touched my food.

He said a muffled OK.

Quickly she took off half her things then went into the bath where water began to run. Shortly she called for him to turn off the light. He didn't. She waited then came out hurriedly and ran to the wrong switch and turned on one more. Lanky my God she was the female Cosmo! He drew farther back under the sheet. After she got the right one she backed in but stayed on her side. He kept the cover high and didn't move. After some moments she backed immeasurably closer. He moved a little to meet her but had to go slowly so her front would stay away from him and with it her face. She moved again keeping on her left side. He inched forward and they met half way. As they did she tried to turn over but he caught her hip with his right hand and her downward shoulder with his left hand and prevented it. There was only one thing to do and he disappeared beneath the covers completely.

She was shocked and embarrassed but she couldn't see him and it went well enough for awhile and then she stopped him. Later while she slept he approached her back again and tried to deal with her. She purred but prevented him or couldn't help and they both slept until dawn when he awoke and relieved himself washed and brushed his teeth and shaved then got back into bed before she saw him. When she awoke he hid under the covers till she too became aware of her need for the bath and left. When she returned he was ready for her and was on top before the horror hit.

My God she said with him working away You're a Frog!

Oui Madame I have lie to you when I say I will be a Prince in the morning.

He turned his head and put his hand over her eyes while he tried to continue. She struggled at first and then let him and then stopped him and wanted to talk. He was still working and did not want to talk: *Copulo Ergo Sum*. But Monsieur she said This is most Existential! She repeated herself in French in case he did not grasp it and he concurred. Delighted she began almost to participate. To keep it totally existential he would not let her look at him. It went well until her courage failed her: she threw off the covers but then would not look back but took her clothes and went into the bath. When she came out she snatched up her purse and left. Then he realized he should have looked for her passport to learn her name. Too late then: gone forever.

So he finished a more careful ablution and went to the Pam Pam for breakfast and then wandered down to the St. George V Church and stared at the mink-clad kidneys of the first-rate girl in front of him. The cleric spoke for the benefit of those who'd not been back for a while of how things were in New York City: service was slow at a watch repair shop he said until they learned who he was.

After lunch he went to a museum and walked along the Seine and then took a late train back to La Beauce Airplane Base with his purchase.

PLAN DE PARIS À VOL D'OISEAU

Years later I re-find you, like a glove
with no mate, old souvenir – I who love
all maps: who lived there then? What did they do?
Where are they now? This asked, I stare at you.
What I think I'm looking for is the place
they meet: **maps measure time as well as space.**
Thus all charts, extended, connect in one
plan galaxies and village plats, head bone
to toe. Look at any, you see them all:
one state shoulders another, borders fall
off, then elsewhere rise, and these too are gone
with the ink still wet. Nowhere is twice drawn,
all our roads are written on palimpsest
where red arterials score tallow flesh,
where cities do their dance, and capillary
country lanes end, blue veins at last gone dry.
This surely is the sense in which "The past
is not over yet, it's not even past."
Tate said Scott Fitzgerald could hardly wait
to get home to paper so he could write
down and make real something that had happened;
and somehow he could find within his pen
the ink of truth. Faulkner made a county,
Yock (unpronounceable), Mississippi.
These too had sought that once somewhere event

from which to which by which all roads make sense.
(Else all points in time are equidistant
from me: ego – εγώ – εγώ ειμι.)
Jerusalem or Minneapolis,
it's much the same, with each map the center
then, afloat in a meaningless cancer,
and one belle isle the most you can hope for.
Which may be enough – to know one harbor,
to have one plan that's never out of date.
Which might be what Scott meant when he met Tate
and while grinning and shaking hands, polite,
asked, "How do you like sleeping with your wife?"

VI

It was late but he checked in on Grisby to see how he was doing and maybe to do a little work on Marianne himself. Gris let him in and he went over to where she lay with her left leg off: the homemade prosthetic device had been worked in on Saturday and was in place except glue on some of the restraining straps was not fully dry.

He had done a good job there apparently.

Do much in Paris JP? He said no: went to the opera and a church.

And your girlfriend?

I have no girlfriend.

No? You go to Paris every weekend and you don't have a girlfriend there? What do you do with your time? Why go?

He bent over to attend to a detail of his work. Grisby had travel posters on his walls but had not been to those places. Not yet: he had often said he planned to go.

I eat a good meal go to the opera or see a ballet if I can get in on Thursday. That sort of thing.

I don't believe you JP but sometime I'd like to go in with you: take a few pictures?

Pictures?

Sure he said: You know the Etoile the place dee la Concorde and the fountains maybe the Seine. Pictures. I'll drive and you can show me the way. Sometime.

Sure. He took out the wig and put it on Marianne who suddenly looked a lot like Raggedy Ann. I'd better comb it he said but I don't have a big toothed comb. Grisby said try a small toothed one then. He did and made some progress. With the eyelashes she began to look like a model or a normal woman in shock. They're too long he told Grisby and got scissors and took a little off. I liked them the way they were Grisby said.

You have no taste: probably go to Pigalle instead of La Madeleine.

Neither one JP.

Where then?

Right here he said and patted Marianne's lower abdomen and then began to fool around. Presently he began to look distressed. What's the matter Gris? Cat got your tongue? No he said But it's got my middle finger.

They worked on it for some minutes and Grisby began thinking maybe they ought to call for professional help.

An MD Gris? Which one? Burger? He's the gynecologist isn't he?

Grisby meant Bowwow the engineer: wears striped ties with checked shirts. He would see is as a Problem and try to Solve it. And would ask no questions. Simon agreed and said the fellow was protected by his PLV.

Which was?

Powerful Limited Vision: it enables him to overcome obstacles by being unaware that they're there in the first place.

So they called him. Bowwow had started a class but quit when Shaw called him a Logic Machine on Legs. The engineer said it all depended on the Premises: he knew what the professor was spouting wasn't Science and he doubted that it was Social. So he dropped. He was a tallish slender blue-jawed fellow with a crump of black hair who had run track in college and boxed and played football. Only when intellectually engaged did he get hot. When he got there he told Grisby to put in two or three fingers. Grisby did. It worked. Was he a doctor too?

Bowwow said he read a lot. Anyway I had it spring-loaded so you had to expand the spring.

Grisby told him to keep quiet about what he had seen and the fellow said Sure. He assured them that Science and its practical offshoots were morally neutral and practitioners were not responsible for what others did with their work: Even if you lose a war: consider von Braun he said Who was not at all unique – all the nations tried to capture in order to hire him and his ilk. The engineers got jobs but Hitler's Führer für Rassenschaft was hanged – *he* was a sort of Social Scientist – and Pound was put on the Funny Farm. Thus Arts and Humanities people are thought crazy and Shaw's types get dispatched and my type get jobs. I prefer my type. They were to call if they needed further assistance.

Simon took the wig off Marianne and fluffed it and put it in the closet.

Busy day coming up said Grisby. Help me put her back in the closet and we'll do some more on her tomorrow night. You smoke cigarettes JP? No? Why? Because I'll need a small piece of cellophane – you know: the way we used to glue it to the balsa on model airplanes for cockpit glass in WW2? But no matter I'll get some on my own. See you in the AM.

He went down the hall and saw that Shaw had moved his Knight to King's Bishop Three. He thought a moment and then moved his own Knight to Bishop Three: it was coming nicely. Then he went back to his own room and slept. The green-eyed woman came again in silence. She scowled at him and asked him if he knew what was wrong with him. H was about to say that he hadn't asked when she told him *You think too much!* And then she was gone.

Cholmondelay was sullenly at work the next morning when Simon got to the orderly room and the First Sergeant was happy to have it so. In his office Simon hacked along on **The Outsider** alternatingly with the Social Sciences text Shaw had assigned until it was time for the work of the day. He looked over the Morning Report very carefully indeed and checked to see that all figures balanced and then after fifteen minutes he signed it and took it back to the Clerk. Then back to the books. At lunch he ate quickly and then went to a dry feeder ditch in back of the BOQ and crouched down out of sight and then lay back on a grassy part. There were a few tadpoles hurrying about also doing nothing in the small bit of the shallows left: they would be happy to hear of rain. Did they ask after Meaning?

He would have been pleased to have stayed there a long time and even to live that way. Except for winter and the need for food and clean clothes. With his head down he could not see the long flat buildings and the telephone poles. You had to pay your way somehow: with that much managed one could escape. The Air Force would pay his way if he could stand another fourteen years but what would be left of him at that time? Driving in first gear. What would be left of second gear if it was not used? To say nothing of third. On the other hand who was he to expect so much? No one. Yet he thought it would be nice to get something anyway.

When he got back to his office he found he had a letter. It was the first one he had received in a month and in fact the one from a month before was from **The Wall Street Journal** and was not exactly personal: Grisby trying to be helpful had sent in his name. But this was in a blue envelope and was handwritten. With French style handwriting but according to the shape of the letters not by someone well educated or much educated at all. He did not open it immediately: orphans do not get much mail. It was not voluminous but it was personal and from a female and addressed specifically to him. There was a return address somewhere south of the Seine in an area that he seldom went to. St. Denis.

It was from someone named Monique. Cholmondelay's Monique: *Dear Lt Simon if you give Airman Cholmondelay back his pass I give you one quickie free. Monique.* Monique. She was an EM's whore so it wouldn't do. But why? Because Officers and EMs ate at different parts of the Mess Hall and wore somewhat different uniforms and lived apart and used different whores. It was becoming a good day: he had got a personal letter and had solved an intellectual problem. He stored the letter for safe-keeping.

Happily there was Officers' Call that afternoon. Nothing would happen there but it would kill the day for him and for everyone else who wasn't flying. Which was most people. The next day there was a Wing Staff Meeting to which he as Commander of Wing Headquarters Squadron would go and that would take care of another day. He told the First Sergeant where he would be and left it open as to whether he would return which of course meant he would not.

Colonel Mousse spoke of something or other (about how complaining airmen were happy whereas complacent ones were not) and there was other talk and finally Chaplain's Call. If it was Ratty then they would hear again what a brilliant man Aristotle was and how bad it was for Americans to swear as they did. Ratty didn't mind excremental swearing but it went against his grain to hear Jesus tossed about. But today was Laufer.

He began with a terrible joke at which someone over-laughed so much that others began to join in and Laufer began to form a false impression of himself. The one about from dust we come and to dust we go and the little kid saying there's someone under the bed either coming or going. It was Longbow who was laughing. In time it became clear that the son of a bitch was drunk. (Ratty would let that pass.) Laufer in full flush began to talk of why some people thought the Lord's middle name was one that began with H: he had often heard it he said as an expletive (Jesus H. Christ) and probably so had others among them. Amen said Longbow and a Negro officer Simon didn't know had to fight back a guffaw. Jesus H. Christ said Laufer and Simon looked around to see if Ratty was there. He didn't find him. First they were told where the Chaplain had seen it of late: someone had autographed a picture in a young officer's room. No said Longbow and Yes said Laufer Yes indeed. Amen brother said the Negro officer and Colonel Mousse looked at him till he was quiet.

Who did it asked Longbow fighting mad. Laufer said he didn't know. The group was large and in the crowd he couldn't tell who was speaking and the Colonel who was at the other side couldn't either but he was looking. Simon began to grow apprehensive for Longbow. It appeared mysteriously one night said the Chaplain.

A miracle said Simon softly but it was heard by many. It was murmured about till finally the Chaplain had to address it and he said No No: Jesus of Nazareth not Jesus H. Christ.

Jesus H. Christ? It was the Negro officer again.

Yes said the Chaplain. But about the H. It was all a confusion over the three letters that abbreviated the name of Jesus: it should be Iota Eta Sigma (looks like IHS) but sometimes it comes out JHC and naturally the ignorant assume the first letter is for Jesus and the last for Christ.

But who signed it? The Negro officer was not smiling now and was doing a beautiful job.

His neighbors hushed him and Laufer continued to rotate his head right and left just as they taught him in homiletics class. The sunlight on the while-blond hair made blank patches like scurf appear and disappear.

Simon turned off listening and idly looked around. At least he had learned something. Hoop was hanging on every word: he too had been grounded but for some sort of psychological deficiency and not for anything physical like his own. Hoop simply couldn't take the stress. The signed Jesus picture no doubt didn't help much and hearing Jake Segal play Boola Boola on the tuba was no great help either. But Segal flew and most nights wasn't there to serenade.

Still Hoop had taken over the Supply Account when Simon was made Commander of the Squadron and had done an excellent job with it: nothing was too petty or minute for him whereas Simon had lost a C-47 and a fire engine. To be sure they could be seen but he hadn't the paperwork to prove them his. But Hoop found it.

Girls he couldn't find. Hoop got letters from girls: lots of them. From some Evangelistic source or other he'd get their names and write them and once or twice a girl had come over to meet him and once or twice he'd gone back to meet them. But that always ended it: not one of them wanted to marry him.

Segal wasn't there. Nor was Grisby. But Jan Gooley was. She was sitting properly and trying to show respect for a clergyman who however heretical at least was worthy of decent treatment because of his office. Simon would ask her to pose for him again. She had done so before but being very flattered by it she kept the picture. This time he would keep it and use it for fine points on touching up Marianne. He stood up and backed toward the side door so he could get his pad and pencils before Officers' Call ended and Jan got away.

When he got back people were coming out but he didn't see Jan among them. She could have gone out earlier or out another door. Quickly he looked inside and there she was talking to Chaplain Ratty her own man. So he was there after all. Possibly consulting him on points of error in Laufer's opinions.

There was a chair extra in the group and he took it and was welcome. Ratty's remaining hair was an irritating red and not a deep thick satisfying auburn like Jan's and his eyes watery blue not her clear feline green. She smiled and showed a flock as white as sheep fresh sheared and every one a twin. Oh that her young roes or grape clusters were twins and Oh the heap of wheat! Someday he would find out. Well you know how the Jews are said Ratty and then acknowledged him.

I'm not Jewish he said. Jan and the Chaplain both knew he went to Protestant services though as an orphan he ought to be Catholic. We were talking of the airman who bought the old limousine to drive troops to Paris Jan said: He makes three trips each way every Saturday and Sunday. Ratty drank from his beer: You know how the Jews are he said. Simon said he approved of Airman Smart's venture. My name is Jewish he said Or at least it often is. But not in my case since they gave it to me at the orphanage: they got me on Simon and Jude's Day. Ratty nodded: he knew when that was. Jan didn't let on whether or no. The Chaplain excused himself momentarily. Where's he going? Jan blushed in reply and he said Oh then he'll be back. She said she hoped so. But tell me she said Why weren't you ever adopted out? Didn't they get you young enough? I mean I'm told that if you're not a young one then you don't get taken: you were never taken?

I was taken on a trial basis he said By a very nice older couple. Oh she purred at the goodness in humankind. They had a nice big white house with while columns on it. Or so it seemed then: I made a special 500 mile detour and went back to look at it before I came overseas and saw it was only an ordinary home and the porch was maybe four or five feet deep but it seemed immense when I first saw it. She laughed at how rooms got smaller as you got older. She was 5' 9" if she was an inch. So you grew up in a big white house? Or what seemed to be one?

No he said I didn't: I was getting along pretty well I thought in school and with them and learning how to used a knife and fork properly and not to talk with my mouth full and all that when one day I came home from school and my bag (cardboard) was on the front porch and my jacket was laid across it and the door was locked. That was the first I knew I hadn't made it. Then a cab came and took me back.

Jan's lovely mouth was open and she was trying to say something but she couldn't.

That was when I was eight maybe seven. It happened five more times. They never kept me more than a month: old people young couples religious or atheist Liberals or Conservatives I never made it. Never found out why. He poured the Löwenbräu the waiter had just brought and drank some and looked up to see her eyes were swimming. He hadn't intended that. She excused herself and ran off but left her purse then came back to snatch it up.

Then Ratty returned and waved him back down from his agitation. I heard that he said: She'll be back. He lit a corn cob pipe and studied Simon: Is it true what you told her? He said it was. Ratty nodded: Well you have a home now right enough. And not a bad place: I've been in fifteen years myself and if my Order doesn't yank me out will stay at least five more. By which time it will be a new Air Force he said When the WW2s and the people who got recalled for Korea and stayed in are out or going out: it'll be all college boys like you Simon in the Officer Ranks. It'll be different to be sure.

He said he wasn't yet a college graduate but he was working at it: taking a course from Shaw just then. Oh yes said Ratty: The Alcoholic. Has a cat? Social Sciences is it?

That's it: the cat's an alcoholic too. Indeed? Yes indeed: the Professor is trying to prove Free Will or some such: if the cat can quit so can he.

Well he's not much along toward quitting is he said Ratty drawing first on his beer then his pipe: I see him every time I'm here.

Then he's here at least as often as you are.

Ratty knocked back more beer and agreed.

Then he told Ratty about the experience on the ceiling and asked him what it meant. Seeing himself in two places he meant.

It means you have a choice. You are indeed privileged to have been given that insight. You are free to choose: that's what it means.

He didn't see how that was so if God knew. Ratty said Simon was free and to leave the mystery to God who could handle it better. But don't forget that Revelation trumps Reason or you'll be like the French who thought otherwise: though Reason indeed supports Revelation.

He had no idea what the priest was saying but said only Is that so? Ratty nodded that it was. Even in France: France is the Oldest Daughter of the Church he said and then winked and added But unfortunately she's a prostitute!

Jan came back and stood beside him smiling down. Do you want to dance she asked. Music he had been aware of was coming from a juke: Jan had put money in. Ratty excused himself and got up to leave and winked at Simon over Jan's shoulder as he left. She was a real slugfoot but it hardly mattered. Yes she said when he asked her yes she would be glad to pose. So when her quarter was up they went back to their table and he drew her full face and then in profile and once in three-quarters from both sides. He used colored pencils to fill in the full-face one. When you get out of the Air Force she said and want to finish college why don't you go to Catholic University? She was going to do graduate work there in Nursing. He wasn't getting out. Oh.

But maybe he could try for an ROTC tour there if he could complete the degree first by taking courses with Shaw and the like. She purred. They rose to dance some more.

Then he was tapped on the shoulder. Just the time for someone to break in. No it wasn't that said Longbow it was just that he heard by the grapevine that he'd got an interesting letter that day: did he intend to use it? No. Then could Longbow have it? Certainly. He gave it to him and Longbow went off smiling after nodding thanks to Jan for putting up with the interruption.

Is he a relative Jan asked. No: why? He looks a lot like you she said. He could be your twin. Same eyes height hair everything. Then thoughtfully she laid her cheek against his and began arhythmically kicking his shoes with hers.

HOW ODD OF GOD

To choose the Jews wrote Ogden Nash but maybe He didn't: maybe *they* chose *Him*. The unwritten word is as smoke (as so finally is that which is written) but the Hebrews wrote down their words and furthermore did so over a period of time which is unique since most books of religion are more or less one-shot affairs but not that of the Jews. (Hebrews before the Babylonian exile and Jews after but no matter.) What they discovered is that in religion a+b does not equal a+b but rather that a+b = a+b+c: when **a** tells his story to **b** then the commonality of the revelation leads to the joint discovery of **c**. If a group (such as the Jews) keeps up that sort of scribbling for a long enough period of time then (if God is indeed revealed through acts in History) this group will discover something of what that pattern is.

This pattern is called Theism: it is the idea that a God outside of History is acting *in* History. The world is His novel.

It well may be then that, as it were, Jews forced the hand of God: if He was to be known at all (again assuming the way God is known is through certain recorded acts in History) then it would have to be through the hands (the writing hands) of those who kept records. Made notes. A more standard view among believers of course in that God chose Jews to keep records. Maybe or maybe not but it comes to the same thing.

Also of course the selection of property awarded by God has something to do with it since Israel's location guarantees anything but a life of quietude: theirs is the land bridge that connects Africa and Asia Minor and hence both to Europe and Asia. A drôle choice since it makes it mile for mile the most precious territory in the world. God has a sense of humor?

The Book we are told begins with Exodus when they got out of Egypt and into Palestine and they then began to consult Oral Tradition for a reason for their being enslaved (why would God allow it in the first place?) and found it in his promise to Abraham. That Land Was Their Land. God did not like Canaanites and their farmer morality but liked the Israelite sheepherder morality: jealous Cain killed Abel and thus Israel was proper in taking Cain's land — there had to be a locus for that History. And so Theism began.

VII

He went past Hoop's door to check on the Sallman Christ he'd autographed and it was still there signed as before. The door was open also to the latrine joining Hoop's room to Laufer's and he poked his head in to Hoop's room to see if it was there where odd noises were coming from and then into the latrine but it wasn't Hoop it was only the Chaplain sitting on the pot and making faces like an Upper Class New Yorker (Cosmo) trying to talk: constipated again. He had heard of Laufer's complaint. Well he said Off to class: going to hear Shaw hold forth on something or other. Laufer past strangled tonsils acknowledged that and said he was going to the movies. Oh. He left and pulled the door to behind himself.

Through Shaw's open door he saw the set illuminated and still on the steel desk and sitting in the yellow glow of the lamp as in an ominous late Van Gogh. Shaw had moved his Queen's Knight to Q2: quickly he countered his bishop to Kt5 and left it as quiet and still as he found it. Then to class.

If Laufer was indeed going to the movie that would mean he was going to see the horse race thing again since there wouldn't be a new flick for two more nights. He went on to class in the Quonset hut area built especially for the Education Program staffed mainly by civilian cookie pushers. The teachers the University of Maryland either provided from the States or else certified from locals who were French or else American military. Shaw was from the States and supposedly was well qualified. He got a seat next to Kate Forney who had one real and one glass eye though he was not sure which was which and he hated to stare too long. She was one of the Available nurses.

Forney leaned over and whispered into his ear The handsomest man in the room has his fly open.

He looked down and saw his wasn't and she giggled. Maybe fifteen years older than he she had silver hair with black brows and lashes and looked good: Longbow said her hair was black as coal somewhere else too.

Shaw came in looking one sheet to the wind and put a big brief case on the desk from which he removed a wind-up clock to tell him when it was time for a break and then dismissal. Then he unloaded a manila folder with his notes in it then a couple of books and finally what looked like a wad of old rags but really was his cat. The cat lay where deposited and Shaw belched softly but thoroughly and began. The problem he said Is that man is born free but is everywhere in chains. Or so we are told. So we are told that man was born free: we can see plainly enough that we are all in chains. You do see that we are all in chains don't you? There was no response. Well he said At least you perceive that *you* are all in chains eh? No response. No? Then why are so many of you in uniform? Shaw looked at Simon to see if the lecture was on target and satisfied that it was he continued.

When we speak of socially-acquired evils he said We are making a redundancy: saying the same thing twice. Man is Born Good (Man Free of Society that is) so Evil (so-called for lack of a better name) comes from

Society. Since man is Born Good it must be that this lack of freedom comes from this construct we call Society. It behooves us therefore to study this complex penal institution we have built for ourselves to languish in: we should learn how intricate are the chains we have fashioned for ourselves to try to dance in. So. Shaw acknowledged Simon's upraised hand. Yes Lt Simon?

If man started Good as you have said (Yes said Shaw) then how did Good Men ever manage to build what you call the mess of Society?

Shaw laughed: You will lead me too soon into demythologizing he said When most of you aren't even aware of the myth itself. But it began when one man said something was his and no one else's and everyone else believed him. It has to do with Private Property. And what is the most Basic Form of Private Property?

Marriage said a voice from the back. He had not known Longbow was enrolled but since the class was only a couple of weeks old so he might have missed because of his flying duties.

Just so said Shaw who was stroking his cat. In response the cat began to snore. We have a sterling example (to use an apt phrase) in the English novel **Pamela** by the eighteenth century writer Samuel Fielding of how this sort of thing works.

Richardson said Forney: Richardson wrote **Pamela** – Fielding wrote *Shamela* and **Tom Jones**. She wiped her left eye and he guessed that must be the false one. Maybe her presence explained Longbow's.

Shaw accepted that and thanked her. Forney glowed. Anyway he said It has to do with a Poor But Honest Girl (the phrase is Richardson's) who refuses the attentions of a wealthy lecher until in desperation he asks her to marry him: he had already failed at seduction and rape. She claims to refuse him on Christian grounds though she never goes to Church and she refuses the hand of a Vicar (who in indeed Poor But Honest) and she ought to tell the lecher to go to Hell: but she is a Capitalist who intends to make a Long Term Capital Gain Investment and until that (Marriage!) happens she will let no man dip into her Principal! It is when we are at our most crass that we pretend to be most noble.

At the break he learned that Longbow had indeed been gone from one or more sessions because of flying and he was explaining this to Shaw who seemed either to understand or else not to care. Perhaps Longbow needed the credits to keep from being riffed: all reserve officers who wanted to stay in feared a Reduction-in-Force that could cause them either to seek civilian employ or else finish their twenty years as enlisted men. Some held on to permanent enlisted rank against the very exigency so they could maybe be Master Sergeants at least if it happened. He was himself a permanent Staff and soon could expect Tech.

After class he asked Longbow about it at the Club: worth it to stay in with that over your head? They settled under the red lights as Longbow affirmed that it was. He said he liked flying very much: what was hard was when you had to land. It was OK so long as you didn't have to land.

Shaw joining them overheard: Do you have another specialty Lieutenant? Something you can do besides fly?

Football he said I play football. As long as I can throw a block or a pass I'm OK. I'm hardly on the downwind leg though. Shaw said it was good he could play well enough to be important that way: flying was not enough and Simon here had the right idea to get out of it as soon as possible. He protested that he had not wanted to get out of flying it had just happened. No matter said Shaw Just so long as it happened. Kate Forney joined them. This made Longbow happy but not Simon because it meant Jan Gooley would stay away since the two nurses were not of the same sort: Available and Not Available. Forney winked her good eye at him though.

We shouldn't have to do anything else in the Air Force Longbow said It's what the Air Force is for. People with other specialties are here to support us – we're not here to support them.

Shaw had been busied with setting a saucer of vodka on the floor for his cat but now he was up and straightening his tweeds. Yes you are he said Though it is your only function: science doesn't exist so that business might use it but heaven help that science which had no business use. Or military use. The president of a chemical company must understand business but need not be a scientist. Scientists are hirelings: even as with pilots and on Army bases where I teach it is the same with their combat officers. With Infantry Artillery and Armored Calvary.

This is dull said Forney Can't we sniff armpits instead for awhile?

Cavalry said Ratty sitting in: *I* am a Calvary officer. Anyway you forgot the Communists. Longbow said Father had taken the words out of his mouth. Shaw insisted La Beauce Air Base was there for jobs for the French and for the Americans. Forney said that was OK because we all lived the way the ancient Chinese were said to do: by taking in each other's laundry. Then she begged May we now please all sniff armpits? Ratty smiled benignly at her words.

Shaw talking over all others insisted if the Commies did not exist we'd have to invent them. Ratty asked And they us? Then Shaw added But all Nature cries aloud they do exist! At the same moment the band struck up In Munchen Steht Ein Hofbrau Haus and there rose an immediate an Ein! Swei! Sofa! response. Simon gritted his teeth. The other chaplain appeared and Longbow asked Laufer to assez his vous and Ratty asked him who won the horse race.

The question said Laufer standing Is not who won the race but rather why is there Something rather than Nothing.

If there is said Longbow and Shaw snorted.

If there is said Laufer: Good night all he smiled and then said Lt Simon I was asked by Lt Grisby to give you a message (that's why *I'm* here): he wants you to come by soon and help him with a project. He smiled and left. German said Ratty. Laufer was almost to the door when Mrs Burger caught him. They were out of earshot but it was obvious she was asking him What It Meant.

Ratty saw her and shuddered: she'd already been to him. Shaw asked who she was. A woman undergoing a program in self-education said Ratty: She's about half way there. Longbow kept his head down since Forney was his interest then. She patted Longbow's knee and when he looked up she winked at him. The cat was snoring again. It lay on its back with feet splayed out to the corners of the compass.

Well said Shaw With Mrs Burger we have yet another Intellectual on the campus.

What's that asked Longbow.

The difference between a Businessman and an Economics Professor said Shaw: The one wants to make money and the other wants to understand how money works.

The difference between a Fool and a Damned Fool said Forney.

Simon said the Intellectual was the man who didn't want to have to come to die and realize that he'd never lived.

Is that what Intelligent men do Ratty said: Come to die and realize at last that they have never lived? Yes said Simon.

No said Forney: The merely intelligent never think of it at all – not at death (I've seen a few die) – nor at any other time. And when Intellectuals come to die they also realize that they have never lived at all. She got up and invited Longbow to come and live awhile: Let's take in each other's laundry she said. Longbow looked up then down then silently nodded and swallowed his beer got up excused himself and left.

Simon gave them a few steps lead and then rose and excused himself too in order to go help Grisby with whatever. He realized whom he'd be leaving together. But he would go anyway.

The unexamined life is not worth living grumbled Shaw and his cat slept on. Ratty asked whether it followed therefrom that the examined life *was* worth living. Shaw snarling said nothing was too stupid to be believed.

Even Atheism?

He left them to it. Longbow and Forney were already out the door and Laufer and Mrs Burger were nowhere to be seen. He walked quietly toward the BOQ when he saw an over-age-in-grade Captain methodically crawling across the parking lot on his hands and knees. When he could get up to his hands and knees. Then a Deux Chevaux came around and turned and neatly ran over him and went on. The Captain continued his crawl. On passing him Simon bent over to see if he was hurt but there seemed no sign of it so when the man looked up he saluted him and went back to his room. Thence to Shaw's where he moved P to K3 in response to Shaw's B to K2. Next Shaw would castle: no doubt about it.

Marianne was looking pretty good when he saw her: the gadget was in place and the body stocking on. Grisby had put her wig on backwards but that was easily fixed. Yet something was wrong.

Ah I see what it is Gris: she doesn't have a navel.

Grisby was struck by that. Everyone ought to have a navel. Did anyone not have one?

Maybe Adam and Eve: there's a joke about their getting lost and then hiding in Paradise and God finding them by checking for navels. Michaelangelo put navels on them though (and uncircumcized David) so I guess *you* could leave one off: same difference. Or you could rename her Eve.

Grisby thought he might indeed prefer that name to Marianne. He guessed he could just pop her a smart one in the middle with a ballpeen hammer and that would leave a dent sure enough. But on the other hand it might break through: Better to let her go as is. He asked for help in sitting her up.

Something said Grisby Has to be done. He wouldn't say what. But he did hold up the cellophane from a cigarette pack. It was to cover her orifice from the inside: sort of a ribbon-cutting ceremony.

Why Grisby you're old fashioned.

He mumbled about always having wanted a virgin.

Then they found on uprighting her was that a thin oil was running out of the gadget between her legs and onto the crevice in back. That was not expected: Gris you may have to wait three or four days. Grisby swore and got a rag.

Anyway he said I haven't finished quite with painting her face.

All cats are gray in the dark.

Just as you please. But Grisby couldn't find the source of the leak and ended up stuffing a sock in her while the face got a final touch up here and there. He sat back and smoked a cigar and watched. He was brewing something and waiting for an opportune time to disclose what it was. Finally Grisby asked whether an extra $50 every two weeks would be welcome.

You plan on pimping for Marianne? Or for me to?

No JP be serious: you sell francs every payday do you not? How many? If you move 100 mille you can add fifty bucks easily.

He worked around her eyes trying for the particular green. He wished he had two of Forney's fake ones. OK Gris: how?

The francs you sell at 350:1 that I can buy at 450:1. Maybe more. Sell at 350:1 the 100 mille I buy at 450:l. That'll come to $100 per pay day give or take a few bucks.

I thought you said $50 profit.

I said $50 for you. I buy the francs so I get half.

But you can't sell them without me. Or someone like me who pays the troops and there's no one else you'd trust as much. I ought to get more than $50. I do the work.

But I have the capital: 50-50 is how it goes. OK JP?

He thought about it and put on one last fleck of black in the iris. He had made the pupils wide but made the irises large too. Perhaps larger than they ought to have been. But it looked right. He cleaned his brush. Ok he said It's a deal.

He left and went to Shaw's where he found the Professor had indeed Castled. He moved his own R to B. He looked for Shaw next to advance a Pawn one space: either to QB3 or QKt3. One or the other. And so to bed.

HAD SILICON BEEN A GAS

Said Whistler, *Had silicon been a gas,*
I would have been a Major General.
He flunked Chemistry at West Point. Ike passed.
And painted less well than Winston Churchill,
who also passed: grades aren't big at Sandhurst.
Retired Field Marshals don't become PM
so WSC got out; Ike stayed, cursed
the dullness, but stayed, and greatness claimed him.
Were silicon a gas, he'd have learned it,
continued to mix his syntax, and paint
farms, covered bridges, snow, leaves that turned. Quit?
Once he thought, *Business.* No hero, no saint,
no malcontent, he was our Wellington,
who planned and waited, served, stayed, planned, fought, won.

VIII

The noise down the hall was from two sources: Jake Segal was playing What a Friend We Have in Jesus on his tuba and Hoop was pounding on his door trying to make him stop. Finally Segal quit and then so did Hoop and Simon went into the shower to get ready for the day. Grisby was just beginning to stir and he asked him if he had Marianne's leak stopped yet. No he said in a muffled voice: he was still under the covers. Probably hadn't even looked. When he got to the sink to shave Grisby was just coming in to use the pot and complaining of Bridegroom's Shoulder and Segal had begun again this time with I Come to the Garden Alone and soon Hoop was pounding on his door again.

It occurred to him that Hoop probably thought Segal was the one who had signed the picture. Maybe he ought to straighten that one out. Or maybe not: it would confuse Hoop to think he had troubled in more than one quarter. Not that Hoop was exactly untroubled. Segal was beginning to jazz it up a bit and then abruptly he stopped. The lucky bastard at least would get to spend his day flying somewhere or other. Maybe Athens or taking toilet paper to Nouasseur maybe Ankara. He was Longbow's co-pilot.

At Shaw's he found the professor had made a weak move: he had advanced a Pawn but to QR3. He moved his own Queen to B2 to threaten. It was going as planned.

At the Orderly Room there was quiet except that Cholmondelay was not in place. He looked at the First Sergeant for an explanation who by way of giving it indicated he would follow him into his office. There he told the story: Cholmondelay apparently in violation of the terms of his Article 15 punishment had left the barracks after work and gone to the Beer Club where he had got very drunk indeed. But that was not all.

When he returned noisily to the barracks it was only to find his way to the latrine to relieve himself of Solid Fecal Matter said the Sergeant. Another in the latrine at the time said Cholmondelay showed gratification on his face on making it to the latrine and lowering his pants and voiding just before it would have been too late. But he had forgotten to take down his drawers. In divesting himself of that mess he made a greater one and the First Sergeant had him in there even then cleaning it up. Did the Lieutenant wish to comment? Yes: bring him in at 1030 for another Article 15. The Sergeant smiled: this time it would be a stripe.

He read in **The Social Contract** until time to sign the Morning Report and then it was time for Cholmondelay. He had nothing to say in Mitigation Extenuation or Defense and accepted the reduction from two stripes to one with no comment. He received also with equanimity the good news that the terms of the earlier Article 15 (restriction to the duty area except for food or church) were now relaxed having been superseded by the later punishment. Dismissed he saluted and left. Then it was time for a PX run and Grisby on being phoned was willing.

He asked whether there was anything especially illegal about selling francs at the unofficial rate. Well said Grisby the French say it's not legal but they make no real effort to stop it and practice is what counts. Possibly the USAF has a rule against it but why ask?

Indeed. He said no more except to ask when they could begin.

Next payday said Grisby: I already have the francs.

You were pretty sure of yourself weren't you? No he said Pretty sure of you. Anyway I could have used them myself.

At the PX they found nothing of particular value so far as buying went until he suggested that Grisby might want to feminize Marianne by buying her some perfume: You know put a little on each breast a dab behind each ear and one each on the pulse at the wrist and on either side of the Promised Land.

She doesn't have a pulse said Grisby.

Maybe not but it's still feminine. Get her something good: Shalimar or what's this? It was Ma Griffe and Grisby liked it. He sniffed and agreed that was the one. Grisby wanted him to go halves on a small bottle but was refused unless they went halves on other matters so Grisby paid it all. Unlike good department store practice the stuff for sale wasn't arranged according to mood or displayed to encourage a particular fantasy. It just sat there heaped under naked fluorescent lighting. Made it tawdry. Or what was the better word? Meretricious. He tried the notion on Grisby who did not know the word or concept though of course he could not have the one without the other. Grisby shrugged it off.

Silly to buy such stuff for a mannequin anyway.

Market Is Never Wrong said Grisby.

Meaning what?

That if there is a market for something (or if a market can be created for something) then Sell It. Otherwise you get into Planning: what we will produce for whom and what they will by damn need and want and like.

But one had to plan for a market did one not?

True JP but it is the Market that decides by the choices it makes whether the planning was successful and not the Commissariat. A better system believe me: if only we could bomb them with Sears catalogs.

That may well be he said and they left with Grisby's purchase.

He skipped lunch after he countered Shaw's R to K with a B to Q3 and spent the entire hour in the ditch behind the BOQ where he was not visible. The tadpoles still wanted water but some were growing legs and seemed to have much less tail than only days before. Most of them looked even so like black sperm wriggling purposefully or at least determinedly. Determined by themselves each of them to succeed (at being frogs at last and leaving frog eggs behind to carry on the fight) or determined by powers without? So long as it was determined it came to the same thing. And ultimately back to Laufer's assertion that all axiological questions led soon enough to the Big *Why?* Why is there Something rather than Nothing. Or as Longbow said maybe Nothing was what there was. Ho hum.

With his head down the engines' noise was less pervasive and a tree or two gave shade. Why had they not been cut down with the other trees? Too much out of the way perhaps. It gave him an idea for Wing Staff Meeting that afternoon: instead of No Report he would suggest they plant trees. If that went well he could suggest putting the telephone and other communication lines underground. La Beauce could be made it not beautiful at least more humane. He felt determined as any tadpole: he had something of worth to do.

A large old well-built farm house and outbuilding that were even then being demolished over the ridge of the ditch had only the large chimney still remaining. It had the date of its erection set in black stones within the greyish white ones: 1776. That wasn't old for the French and he supposed the building ordinary enough though in the States it would be a classic.

Meanwhile Professor Shaw had taken his Pawn and he in exchange took Shaw's. First blood. The game was significant no matter whether frogs or farmhouses were. Games were for avoiding making embarrassing questions about Significance. Pointless questions rather. Thus games became quite complex and men invested much of their personalities therein. In any case their own chess game was a good one since they were evenly matched: no one could play well against an inferior opponent and only a little better or worse than an equal.

He went back to his office to wait for the meeting and on the way passed Queenie Compson the librarian but she seemed puzzled as he went by: didn't know him for sure but felt she ought to. Well she was drunk the night he carried her home. He spoke anyway and she made a fleeting smile but nothing on the order of the eye-closer that Southrons usually gave in genuine greeting. He would reintroduce himself as occasion permitted but would have to be delicate about it. He poured himself a cup of coffee in the day room and stayed in his office and read until time to leave. In a Manual he perused by chance he found the statement that in the USAF a Squadron was the smallest Self Contained Unit: it could feed itself move itself and fight. Then it was added parenthetically that man was not a self-contained unit. Odd inclusion. He then stopped off at the latrine. As he stood there a female voice greeted him from behind the stall doors: it was a French National the one who ran the TB clinic for other French who worked on the base. They parked her mobile unit outside Headquarters Squadron building so she plugged into their electricity and came to their latrine for relief. He greeted her in return then shook himself and zipped: how could she recognize him? By his feet? Or perhaps the Silver braid on his cap showed to her over the door. He was glad he hadn't flatulated as he was on the verge of doing. And what must she think of the ignorant graffiti scribbled on the stalls? Obscenity was OK but no vulgarity. Then she flatulated.

The meeting was not yet convened and as the lowest ranking officer indeed the only Lieutenant (and there were only a couple of Captains) he was told to wait and call the room to attention when the Base Commander entered. But Colonel Mousse though on the edge of entering was standing and talking with another Colonel: which of them or whose father or grandfather laid down the biggest turds. Mousse insisted his grandfather could do four-footers every time that were four inches in diameter and the other said his father beat that every time. Mousse denied it but then turned to enter and the room was called to attention.

There was business which got taken care of first and then it was time for each unit to report. Most had nothing and then when it was time for Wing Headquarters Squadron he swallowed his heart and said he thought he had an idea for base beautification. Indeed it might relate to the morale problem that the Colonel said a couple of weeks before that he thought the base had.

Well said a Lieutenant Colonel Well?

Plant trees said Simon and then if feasible put the communications lines underground. Most of the officers looked blank. It would make for a more pleasant atmosphere if there were not the visual obstruction of the lines he said And also if there were the obstruction of trees.

Put telephone lines underground said the Colonel?

Yes sir it would save money. They're easier to fix when they break being where they are but they break much more easily where they are. It would be more economical to put them under in the first place. And better for Defense.

Lieutenant the French are going to reclaim this base in ten years or rather they're going to claim it then depending on how you look at it: we built it for them so that's a claim not a reclaim but since it's their land to begin with maybe it is a reclaim. Anyway there's no point in planting trees. The Colonel smiled: We'd plant them and they'd have to rake the leaves.

The world was not a desert when I was born into it he said and then felt ice in his veins which quickly thawed when he saw none of them understood.

Leaves are the problem said the Colonel we don't want all those leaves to have to rake. As for putting poles underground that's absurd.

Just the lines sir not the poles.

All right he nodded All right: we'll consider it. Next.

They continued on around the long black rectangle of table and the MD (Burger) made his noises and the Chaplain reported and Base Supply and so on. Then it was time for the Intelligence report and Cosmo suddenly appeared and the Chaplain and the MD were excused. But before he left Burger sent a note around the table to him. See me at 1600 it said.

Cosmo looked seriously around the room to see if anyone there was not cleared and then he flipped up the cover on a large series of maps and began to talk of troubles in the Near East: big doings coming up in Turkey but we were on top of them. A coup was on but those to be couped knew of it although they didn't know that we knew: if they did know and we didn't know that they knew that we knew well then things might get very sticky indeed and uh we shouldn't plan any long leaves for the next week or two but he was sure we soon would know if they knew we knew that they knew. For the time being a Wait-and-See attitude was being adopted. Cosmo knit his brows and appeared very serious though very competent. The Colonel thanked him and the Major in charge of Intelligence nodded for him to go and Cosmo ducked his head for the door frame and left. Cosmo did not quite need to duck.

After the meeting Simon went back to his office and made out the duty roster for Officer of the Day for the next two months putting himself as far back as he decently could. Then it was time to go see Burger. When he got to the Hospital he found Burger himself right in the central hall holding forth to Nurse Forney that all female maladies were centered on one place. Captain Forney said well hers wasn't it was her eye. Burger told her to come see him in a few minutes that he would attend to Lieutenant Simon first.

Where do you hurt she asked him. Nowhere he said It's a different matter. He followed Burger into his office. Burger was not usually in command of the Base Hospital but the Flight Surgeon who had been in charge had to be taken away when he developed DTs. Until Shaky was back Burger had it. And loved it. He sat in Shaky's big chair behind his big desk and smoked his big cigars. He was going to give Simon some advice about what it was like Out There.

He looked out the window but Burger shook his head at him and he saw the MD meant Out There in the Civilian World. It's no different from in here Burger said Except the Pension Rights aren't as good: so don't resign when you encounter stupidity. Believe me it's no different out there and I thank God that the Korean thing came along and I got recalled and it gave me the excuse to stay in. You might get out of the Air Force Simon but you'll never get out of the System: all you'll do is give up your pension rights.

I'm not thinking of resigning sir.

Burger didn't even raise his head to look up. Banal he said It's banal: we can talk about it all we want to but then the talk itself becomes banal.

It's what's wrong with Sinclair Lewis' novels: an exposé of the banal very soon becomes itself banal. He raised his yes: You know Lewis? Simon did not. Burger told him that was OK he could skip Lewis. Or read one but no more: they were all the same.

Well about getting out: you will think of it Simon you will. I've seen bright young officers like you before and sooner or later they get fed up. I know: I was one of them. Lost four years that way and I'd be a Colonel now if I'd stayed in.

I plan to stay in sir.

OK said Burger resting his cigar and at last looking at him full bore. He had white showing all the way around his eyes. One other thing: you heard me talking to Nurse Forney about her problem. She may think it's her eye but it isn't. It never is with women. 75% of a doctor's business is with women even if he's not a GP. Listen Simon this is important whether you stay in or get out: be careful who you marry.

He pushed his chair back and got up. Now I have to see Kate he said and left by a side door. Simon went out the way he came in and saw Forney sitting in an examining room whose door was open. She had on an eye patch. Left eye. He wanted to ask if he could borrow her eye sometimes soon but this wasn't the moment to do so. She smiled at him. So he asked. He just wanted to see it he said if it wasn't too personal. Could he? Even borrow it for a bit? He would show no one. She thought on it without showing offense.

I guess so she said But you can't have it now.

Oh I thought because of the eye patch –

She smiled and stood up and looked down the hall and then took her chart off the door she was waiting beside and reached back and took his hand and led him inside and locked the door. She gave him her nurse's uniform to hang on the tree next to the door. Then a slip came his way. Panties were thrown on a chair. She grunted slightly and was in the stirrups. It was not erotic: a damp wad of black and beneath in a brown fig and then a brown dot lower yet. Her legs had small purple and red rivulets in them and parts of her thighs were marbled. OK she said?

OK what?

Look she said. Wash your hands first. He did and then looked and she said You'll have to open them. Gingerly he did: her eye was there looking out at him.

Presently she sat up and began to arrange a sheet over herself. That she said Is what Burger is going to see when he comes in here: he's looked at a lot of them and now it's time one of them looked at him. He needs it: every one of the bastards has two semester of God in Med School. She was not smiling: They get two semesters because invariably MDs kill people since MDs after all are human and make mistakes so to keep them from feeling bad about it they get told that everything they could possibly need to know that they do know because it has been taught to them so no they do not make mistakes. We nurses call it Two Semesters of God. Put my folder on the door bracket outside when you go will you doll and close the door behind you? She gave him a wink but still no smile. He said he would and did.

Jan was in the hallway passing by when he came out and she saw him put the chart on the door and before he shut the door she something else that made her green eyes go very wide indeed and her red mouth showed forty or fifty white teeth and a baby pink tongue. Ooh JP! She drew in her breath. He took her elbow and led her away a few feet and whispered in her whorled small ear about what was going to happen. She was delighted and giggled with her hands over her mouth until a shock came over her and she grew crimson. He had seen another woman. She ran away down the hall with her faced covered and her heels kicking back at him as she ran with her knees hobbled in the loin-weakening way most women ran and with her bottom shifting starchily from side to side.

His heart was with love three times its normal size when he left and he noticed only casually Cholmondelay in the Waiting Room cradling a bundled thumb. A goldbrick no doubt about it.

Three other nurses he knew slightly but who were ignoring him stood nearby in intense conversation: a pretty one with ash blonde hair the color and thickness of a Kansas wheat field in August if seen from a thousand feet asked the other Did you hear about Meg Ryan? A dark Galway face intensely focused on Blondie: no she had not heard. Nor had a redhead.

Married an Italian said Blondie and Galway's and Red's faces dropped. Blondie waited then said flatly and with finality And there she is.

He passed on and missed the rest but what more was there to say? Catholics. Irish. Married forever. With Jan that might not be so bad.

IX

At the Orderly Room it was confirmed that Cholmondelay had indeed injured slightly a digit and was officially excused to go to the hospital: he had caught it in a filing cabinet drawer. Also it was reported that the Protestant Chaplain's Assistant had the crabs but doubtless had contracted them innocently. That would be Walsingham: a slightly rotund and very clean fellow who looked to be well-cast. Roberts the Morning Report Clerk was ignoring all this and was attending cheerfully to his work. His wife's coming in tomorrow said the First Sergeant at Orly: Roberts has his mind on his stomach.

That's right said Roberts: I'm going to get cabbage cooked three hours and corn bread with no sugar in it and pork chops with white gravy and berry pie oh my. His eyes wrinkled and the smile became general. He really is thinking of his stomach Simon said and the First Sergeant nodded. Maybe that was what marriage was for.

He proposed as much to Grisby as they got the repaired device securely in place and glued. It would take a good while to dry but once it was dry the glue was guaranteed to hold like iron: some new kind of stuff Grisby had heard about. The cellophane was in place and Marianne was a virgin. Well he asked Grisby What about it? Do you think Marianne can cook?

Grisby continued to say nothing but only sat and studied his creation. After a while he was asked whether he felt more like God or Dr. Frankenstein.

Neither one JP: Just wish there were some way to market these. But there's no way.

Maybe you could make up a kit that people could send away for. You know: you send all the parts and they save money by doing their own labor and construction. Handy Man's Delight. Sears used to sell entire houses. That sort of thing. Bowwow could help you with it.

You're missing the point JP: here help me put some clothes on her. He got out two or three sets of underwear and skirts and things. Got them from Plumsby the Medical Staff Officer: they had a shakedown inspection of the medics and took away all of their female clothing. All he told me was that I had to throw it away after I was finished looking at it. Something ought to fit.

Indeed by manipulating straps and things they got a brassiere on her and then easily panties and then a garter belt which they had to unhitch when they realized the panties were for over and not under it and then they added a slip. Nothing matched much but with stockings on she looked pretty good. The Kelly green blouse didn't go with the purple skirt but that was luck. The black and white pumps were a difficult fit and didn't help a lot either but she was dressed. Why do women wear so much gear JP? There ought to be a simpler way of putting themselves together.

Keeps them in their place I think: like having long nails and hair that needs frequent attention. Clothes do the same thing. They used to wear more complex ones than this stuff and besides they had to change them several times a day. If they were ladies. Men too. Kept them in their place by keeping poor people out: like Pharisees and Sinners Laufer said once with rules only the leisured could keep. We still wear ties. To show we don't work with our hands.

Holds your shirt together said Grisby while hoisting Marianne under the arms to put her back in the closet. Simon said women like to attract attention: That's why they do nails hair and stuff. Buttons will do as well as a tie. It's there to show we're not going to do any useful work. Or should I say physical work? Can't swing an axe or run a lathe with a tie on. Say why don't I get her some false nails and paint them? Everything false we add to her than real women add to themselves will go that much further toward lessening the difference between Marianne and her protoplasmic counterparts. Grisby said OK to that.

They bundled up the left-over clothes and he told Grisby he knew just the place to drop them. Hoop's door was locked so he tried Laufer's and found it open. When he called his name the Chaplain through straining teeth told him to come in: on the pot again. He stuffed the things in his wastebasket for the maids to find and cluck over the next day. They would say nothing to anyone official though since that would involve handing over what they had gleaned and none would want to have to do that. I've got a confession to make he said having decided to tell who had signed the Sallman. You got the wrong Chaplain said Laufer with difficulty: Make your confession to God. All I can offer is pastoral counseling.

OK he said: Going to see the horse race film? Last time it's on is tonight.

There followed a low groan and then an assent. Well see you afterwards at the Club maybe. Sorry to hear about Walsingham he said and closed the door behind himself. Shaw's door was open: Shaw had moved a Pawn to Kt4. OK: he would retreat his Bishop to Q3.

At the Club he found Longbow and Segal sharing a table and asked to join them and was admitted. You know said Longbow We ought to get this boy back on flying status Jake and he could be our navigator. Segal said he would drink to that and did so but Simon had to tell them that barring a change in regulations it was not to be. Although he would indeed like it: navigators flew on the average about one week of every four and that would be just right for him.

Rules in the military said Longbow Are made to be waived: you better go talk to someone in Legal and see what can be done. Then Longbow saw something that turned him pale. Simon and Segal both looked to see what it was but all they noticed was Queenie Compson drunk again at the bar. Who's that asked Longbow Up there at the bar? They both said it was Queenie Compton or Compson. Compson said Longbow Not Compton: Comp*son*. Well then said Segal If you knew who she was why did you ask us? Do you know her?

I did he said Some time ago. In another country. But I thought the wench was dead. Say uh he said reaching for his wallet Maybe I'll uh go catch that movie about the fillies and leave you all to finish your dinner together and I'll see you all later. Segal pointed out that Longbow's dinner though ordered hadn't got there yet. Simon here can eat it said Longbow: You will enjoy it Simon. He said his name the French way. I'll even pay for you boy. He left three dollars in scrip and exited quickly and quietly by the side door.

That's not the way to the movie house.

I noticed that said Segal. The band began to assemble behind them and the clarinetist tootled In Munchen Steht Ein Hofbrau Haus and Segal winced but a couple of other diners cheered. The music would not start for some minutes though. The bane of my life said Segal Is bad music.

Really? You don't hear that much good stuff by tuba players. I mean you can't exactly do Flight of the Bumble Bee or Beethoven's fifth now can you?

I can and what is more do. My fiancée and I used to play duets: I with my instrument and she with hers. Hers? Xylophone he said.

I had no idea you were engaged.

I'm not: she died.

Sorry.

It's just as well. Segal picked up his implements to pry into the chop suey laid before him. Longbow had ordered a steak and it looked pretty good although three dollars wasn't quite going to cover it. Still he needn't have left even that much.

Love and Marriage said Segal with his mouth full but no food showing Romantic Love and Marriage my dear sir are not compatible: Romantic (also called Courtly) Love should be ever ascending and should it falter it most often dies and but rarely revives. Further: one should think constantly on one's beloved and no one Good Sir is ever bound by a double love. Also: he who loves sleeps and eats very little (you will observe that *my* appetite is sound) and is constantly jealous although never avaricious. In conclusion: that set of rules makes love possible and even religious but hardly can such love be found compatible with marriage which is a dull and stable and confining and ordinary state leading most often to children and their tending. Such Romantic rules work only if one of the partners will agree to die. Thus I eschew it entirely. He swallowed and bit again. Finally: love flourishes best when it is kept secret and not made public for the vulgar to observe it. Marriage is extremely public. In short I can't hack Romantic Love.

Yet you were engaged and you did love the girl.

Works out only if one of the partners will agree to die before the spell wears off. Priscilla did that. Gracious of her. But ours was not Romantic Love.

Priscilla?

Gagliardo. Old New England family. Pass the sugar please.

A large hand appeared tweed-clad over his shoulder and shoved the bowl roughly toward Segal spilling a third of it. Shaw was loaded. Who's an Old New England family he said seating himself approximately.

Segal's deceased fiancée.

Shaw thought about it a moment or appeared to. Then he cleared or appeared to clear his head: Well out of it he said. Sex and Jealousy is all it is said Russell and then you're in it for life. Enslaves. A married man will do anything for money. Obedient. Can do anything with them then.

Hmmm: maybe we ought to get Cholmondelay married off. But to whom? Ah: Monique.

Segal said he knew him. But he didn't know her.

A lady of the night. French.

Makes no difference who it is said Shaw: Effect is the same.

Probably you could pass her off here said Segal: Was she one of the expensive sorts? Simon shook his head. The band began to play something called Maqué Maqué ma qu'est-ce que c'est or at least that was what it sounded like. The singer was tall and blonde and never spoke French and probably couldn't. She was Swedish. Segal was looking at her with admiring eyes. Shaw even turned about to get her in focus. Not French he said when he turned around. He hailed the waitress and ordered whiskey. Did he wish anything to eat? Raw onions and rye bread he said and was told they would try to supply it. Then he changed his request to vodka. He turned again to the band: She's not French.

Swedish I think.

Segal was interested by that. We're all foreigners here then he said: That's nice. Except of course she's not military. What difference did that make Shaw asked fidgeting for a drink. I don't know said Segal But it's different: when you're abroad you're an alien in more than the legal sense. You don't need to play by the local rules. In fact you can't play by them. In the military you can't play by local rules even in your own country: it's all suspended for the duration of your service. If you're abroad that intensifies it. It's as if everyone were a Jew.

Shaw studied that closely: Hum?

Jews are resident aliens Segal said: Everyone knows that. Home is Israel. Whether you ever intend to go or not. That's why we're so analytical wherever we are: we have a certain detachment a certain perspective.

Shaw dismissed it: Jews are analytical in Israel too. Anyway he said It's your grammar of two tenses (that which is done / that which is yet to be done) that puts you right in the middle. The grammar bred a culture out of your God's demands.

Simon had never studied any language before French and Segal said his Hebrew had only marginally satisfied the rabbi. Shaw said it mattered little but he had to go to his class anyway. You're not coming Simon?

No I'm in your class tomorrow night. Shaw said Oh and gulped his drink wrapped in a napkin his meal and then fumbled out some scrip and launched off through heavy seas.

He asked Segal if he felt Not at Home. Segal was dreaming in the direction of the singer who had begun to notice him and was now and then smiling his way. Huh? At home? Oh no I guess not: permanent alien.

I feel more at home here than in the States. I'm sort of an alien there: no family. Here I'm officially an alien and more at home since my condition is officially recognized for once. Soldiers away from home aren't used to being aliens and some cause trouble because of it but I'm alien at home.

Did you make trouble at home? Segal spoke dreamily as he smiled at the blonde.

No. He wanted to say something more but couldn't bring up what he was trying to ferret out of the junk heap of his mind.

Segal said Ratty had offered it once at Chaplain's Call that we not at home here since it was not our final home: Possibly that was before you were on the Base?

That was exactly what he was trying to bring up! And it was before he got there: Who said that?

Ratty.

No no no: who was he quoting?

Whom? Dunno. Pascal? I didn't buy it: here is at home as it gets.

Then why don't you marry? You know: mow the lawn. Analyze less.

What was wrong with analysis?

Nothing he supposed if one stopped short of the Mrs Burger Syndrome. Segal concurred. Segal studied his fortune cookie: Simon knew what they looked like? No? Women sit on one he said. Simon sighed and thought again of Queenie.

Each woman thinks because she has a cookie she has a fortune hidden in it said Segal Which of course she can't read. So they look for someone who can. If asked we of course lie and say we can but it's written in some pre-Babel tongue and we can't. Then they're disappointed. He paused: once I

♦

helped Priscilla speak in tongues though. He ate the cookie. Once he said It was Pentecost: but I couldn't understand her.

What did his own fortune say?

He pushed the paper over: Seek and You Shall Find. You on for the parade this Saturday Simon? He said it Frenchly.

Damn! I forgot about it. I was going to Paris. Probably I'll have to be Squadron Commander for the march. Merde alors.

Why do you go to Paris Simon? For the opera?

Yes and the good restaurants. Now and then the ballet. Museums. Or just to be there.

Segal nodded: We should have gone in some time together.

We still can.

Wait till after Saturday Segal said: If I pull it off we'll talk about it. Shaw's wrong about the grammar bit by the way: the Chinese are the Jews of the East and they don't have tense at all. But sure: we'll go to Maxim's. He turned away then and after saying of the singer She's back he went away to head her off before she got to the microphone. They talked a bit and Segal signaled to him to count him out for the rest of the evening. So Simon paid his tab and left.

Just as he got out the front door he saw Jan coming back from her own class. A Freshman World Lit sort of thing he'd had elsewhere but which Jan as a nurse missed in her training. She was disturbed obviously but on seeing him cheered considerably. So did he on seeing her. It was Spring and a night of the South Wind a night of the Large Few Stars. She saw that he welcomed her too and she hugged him dropping her book as she did so. When she released him he bent to pick it up but she told him not to: It's trash she said.

He got it anyway and found it was Bulfinch. This stuff has lasted a long time he said and carried it after she refused to take it. She didn't care if he had it though she was not disposed to have it again. Instead she hung on his left arm with both of hers and put her head on his shoulder though it was hardly a descent for her to do so and swung beside him on long and striding legs. How suddenly her mood had gone from frustrated to contented! She said nothing of the book and apparently cared not to. She was bumping his hip with hers.

He wondered whether he should bring it up: Shaw had said women didn't believe in ideas really but only used them as they had to. Shaw said there were no female colossal sillies no Kants or Hegels. And no chess grandmasters. Jan's hair was dark red even in the faint light and it smelled fresh and good. Her breast rose against him though he thought she had not consciously put herself so but only did it because she walked close to him. He was happy.

When they were half way to her BOQ she asked what he was going to do when he got out. Just travel around Yurp for a while? He said again that he didn't know he would get out. Oh she said and continued her long swinging steps and letting her haunch hit him as it would. He recalled cats around the orphanage did that around toms when in heat. All nature was a unity and he was glad of it.

Jude she said Why don't you try to teach ROTC while I go to school and get a Master's?

His stomach clutched but he said OK and she tightened her grip.

At her door she turned to kiss him and in such a way that said he might be asked in. It was not a polite kiss or a playful kiss or a friendly kiss it was a long kiss a kiss of youth a kiss of love. When she was through with it she rocked her chin on his shoulder and sighed and sighed. Her hair was in his face and he knew better but he asked her anyway: why was she so unhappy when he found her? Oh nothing she said. That was behind her. But he asked again and again until it was back with her. It was in class tonight she said: The Professor said some nasty things about a king a Greek king and his wife who uh who oh had an affair with a bull.

Oh. The story of the minotaur: King Minos. And Pasiphaë. What was wrong with that?

She pulled back from him from the waist up and studied him. The Professor wasn't very nice. To bring it up I mean. You know: the girl made a mistake that's all. He didn't need to snicker over it.

Did he snicker over it?

Well I think so. Anyway he brought it up and he shouldn't have.

Everyone ought to know Greek mythology he said And Pasiphaë wasn't a very nice girl.

She glared at him.

Well she *did* sleep with a bull!

Only once! She pushed off from him and without saying good night opened and slammed the door shut.

He cursed himself many times over and then quieted with the thought that he could look forward to Shaw's latest move if the door was open. It was: Shaw had moved B to Kt2. He moved a Pawn to QR4 to prevent Shaw's advancing a Pawn of his own to B4 or 5. Soon it would become bloody and he would sacrifice his Queen if necessary. But he could replace her.

So he went to bed and tried not to think of Jan. He slept but in the last moments of darkness before the break of dawn the redheaded woman seated on a throne came before him with a scowl and disdain and boredom all at once on her visage: You persist in asking questions she said For which there are no clear answers and who cares anyway?

He sat upright and sighed. Then he put his feet to the cool tile floor and went to the toilet to urinate. After that he felt able to return to sleep and did so and forgot the message and the messenger.

BIKINI BEACH PARTY

American culture exists on a continuum, with a set of James Boys at either end.

                                               – Peter DeVries

The scene is one with which we're all familiar:
Sand, beach balls, girls in bikinis, though Annette's
has no bottom. This is her dream, we're in it
and mustn't wake her. Which is why when it's *our*
dream no one snickers, points, or notes us, never,
however shamed we are. The game goes on, boys
and girls in Innocent America, noise
they dance to in the background, sunlit veneer
everywhere. Annette hides, in front at least,
behind a globe of colored wedges, but throws
it when she has to. The water when she goes
to it recedes, it will not cover her beast.
To one side, an umbrella shelters two men
of nineteen-five, the James Boys, Will and Henry:
"**Daisy**," says Will, "**once-born**," to silent Henry.
From far shadows, Frank and Jesse point and grin.

X

On Friday night Marianne was ready for deflowering but Grisby would permit no ceremony of any sort nor did he want a party. It's not as much fun JP if you're married: this is just an affair that's all. An affair about which you had damned well better keep your mouth shut.

They got her to bed and now he wished he'd not made her look so much like Jan. He stood there until Grisby told him to leave: he didn't expect to get to watch did he? Well he had sort of expected to go second. No said Grisby Not tonight: we want to be alone. Or rather I do. Go to the Club. Come back late.

So he left. At Shaw's a Pawn had been moved to Kt5. So. He took a Knight with a Bishop. Which meant Shaw's remaining Knight would take his Bishop and after he advanced a Knight to K4 to prevent Shaw's advancing his QBP then that Knight would be taken and with his Bishop he would take Shaw's remaining Knight. Then a Bishop would be lost but with his Queen he would avenge the loss. Then to the Club.

He had seen Jan every evening since the night she had been so unraveled about Pasiphaë's being harshly judged by the male mentality: All for Love. He had at first been worried that there was a bull in Jan's life but she angrily assured him it was not so. He felt better. About some things and worse about others: for the past few days he had been concerned about the Communists and their attempts at world domination. He had become diligent at work and no longer read books during working hours: instead he called meetings and culled records and sent to the photographer names of officers whose photos in their personnel files were out of date and he counseled career men about their insurance provisions and he was Very Busy Indeed. It was his way of doing what he could to Increase Efficiency and Resist Communist Aggression.

At heart he knew it was Jan: he had to protect her and the children. There were as yet no children and the word Marriage had not even come up: but it was hovering there just outside their reach or vision and when its name was called then it would be Real. He was amazed at what a sleepwalker he had been before at how dead he had been. Now it was time to get serious. And to pick up Jan. Her red hair was the dark rich mop it had ever been and her clear green eyes were glad to see him but Oh my God she was wearing a strong green blouse with a big floppy bow in front and a purple skirt that fit fairly tightly down to the knees. Black and white pumps. Nurses were the female equivalent of engineers and not to be relied upon to know all things. Engineers dressed oddly too. When she looped her arm in his he didn't care.

She had reserved a table for two for them and she snuggled her head on him and said she asked for that kind so no one else would butt in on them. They had hardly been seated and put their orders in though when Jake Segal came over obviously looking for him. The band assembled and the inevitable In Munchen Steht Ein Hofbrau Haus struck up. Where had he been?

In Nouasseur said Jake but he said he met the particular figure they both had noticed earlier that week. He did not understand Jake and certainly Jan didn't but her eyes were following his closely. The singer said tactless Jake That one there. She was out of ear shot but the Swede could not have cared less: I went back to her room the other night with her Segal said now talking directly to Jan And she invited me in. But one thing was wrong: the whole band was there. And she said I could be after them. I talked them into drawing cards and I was fourth.

Jan's nostrils were drawing rapidly in then flaring out and her fair skin was pale. I'll see you later he told Jake And we'll talk about it. Sure said Jake and slapped him on the shoulder and walked off.

Another Pasiphaë he said to Jan But her mistake was more than once. Five times he said counting No six. Jan now was sad: Does everyone have to be depraved.

Not everyone is: the singer is and Segal. The band. Maybe Segal's OK.

He doesn't sound so healthy-minded to me she said and popped the cherry from her whiskey sour behind her teeth then closed her lips on it and thoughtfully pulled out the stem.

Well only once he said. She didn't remember the jest and he was glad of it. Anyway he said You aren't depraved and I'm not. She smiled and swallowed the cherry and put the pulp of the orange slice in her mouth up to the rind. For a moment she had three lips: a red one up and a red one down and an orange one in the middle. Then she pulled out the stripped peel and ashtrayed it along with the stem. Only then did she raise the tart foam to drink. Her nostrils flared again as she took in the alcohol fumes. She sighed and put down the drink. There was froth on her upper lip.

What it does she said Is make us seem dirty. Oh I know we haven't done anything yet Jude but we will when we're mar uh more uh. She stalled out then got started again grabbed the word from the air and pushed it at him When we're married. She looked away. Hearing no protests she turned back toward him: And then it will seem tainted. Oh I don't know. I don't want to think about it.

His feet were nailed to the floor and his hands to the table. Married. Yet his hands and feet did not hurt: it was only that he could not move them.

But Jan was not looking at him any more: she was staring at the front door with widened cat's eyes curious as hell. He looked: it was Longbow with a school teacher he didn't recognize. No she was too young to be a school teacher: you had to have two or three years teaching stateside before you could come over and she was no more than 19 or so. But American. She was a bold thing and enjoying herself. She and Longbow waved to them interrupting his conversation with the girl to do so. They were speaking in French and the girl's accent was gutter Parisian. My God it was Monique. Longbow had taken his chit and cashed it and then some. And on a Friday night at that: he must have done some powerful persuading.

He watched them take a table under one of the lights that shone so brightly within a sharply defined area but not elsewhere: under the white cone they made a bold Hopper painting. He was thinking of that and the American Art History course he had taken when his crucified right hand began to prickle. It was Jan poking at him with the tines of her salad fork. How couth you are he said: One always stabs one's boyfriend with the fork farthest from the rim of the plate. Unless that fork has been soiled of course in which case –

Who is she?

She? Oh I don't know: a school teacher I suppose.

I know them all and she's not from here.

From somewhere else then.

No she whispered She's too young. And besides that she speaks very good French.

She speaks atrocious French. But I think it's native. I guess she's a French girl.

Jan's eyes narrowed: But what is she doing here?

Why not? It *is* France after all. But she didn't care for that sort of sophistry and sat back with a humpf.

He looked over where they were sitting and saw that Colonel Mousse was moving in. Longbow could handle him surely: football players had a lot of leverage in the military. But Longbow was welcoming the Colonel to the table and seemed to have no particular concern about losing Monique's favors. Which he guessed was reasonable enough of Longbow: what claim could one have on a prostitute? And Longbow was not one to get jealous:

Whatever else you do See-mone he had said Do not let the lady make you jealous or you in her power.

Segal was hovering not far from them but Longbow looked ready to move off. And did: Monique waved farewell and the Colonel nodded a sort of thanks and then began to dig in with her. Segal continued to wait. Longbow passed them by on his way to the bar and Simon said I guess you practice what you preach Lieutenant: Don't let them make you jealous.

Longbow stopped long enough to greet Jan and to clap him on the shoulder: That's right young man he said and winked at Jan. You let them get you jealous next thing you are a married man.

With children said Jan smiling.

Worse and worse said Longbow: Flying is fine but you don't want to land. It's OK so long as you don't have to land.

Then you can't have any children Jan said.

Sure you can: I got four or five here and there. He pointed a finger at him and moved off: Don't land See-mone don't land. Jan watched Longbow swing along in his athletic way and then covered both his hands with hers: You're grounded Jude Paul Simon you're grounded. He avoided her level gaze but said his name was Patrick not Paul: James Jude Patrick. For life she said: You are grounded for life.

She snapped her head up and down once in sharp affirmation of the statement: For life. He said nothing but was very happy. Mousse he saw was leaving with Monique and Segal looking challenged was following. Jan noticed not at all. She was beginning to dine with strong but graceful fingers. She didn't know quite how to handle her fork though: unusual in a woman.

After dinner they went over to the area of comfortable chairs and away from the band. Ratty came in presently and seeing Jan headed over to join them. And Shaw seeing Simon did the same. Not especially drunk he was also less than perfectly sober. He had his cat along slumped in a baggy side pocket of his tweed jacket. When he raised a hand to order the torn elbow of the jacket showed below where the patch was coming off: so those weren't there just for effect but to do a job.

He ordered two brandies and a saucer. Ratty told him he was disgusting. Same to you said Shaw. What are you trying to prove said Ratty That a cat can be just as depraved as a human? No said Shaw That a human can be just as moral as a cat. Then he looked at Simon: You at least understand that don't you? My best student? That if this cat can give it up then so can I?

Or anyone?

The cat has no reason said Ratty.

Simon squeezed Jan's hand to get her eye to see if she wanted to leave but she was too partisan to the priest to leave the battle. Angry she was beautiful and fierce and he wondered how her ancestors managed to lose the Battle of the Boyne against Protestants. But Shaw had covered that too: similarly equipped Evangelicals seldom lost to Catholics since they were too neurotically single-minded to do so easily. But Evangelicals now were few.

Of course she has reason said Shaw. He set the saucer on the table near him and while he drank off his own brandy the cat emerged far enough to lap hers. Frenetically. Ratty only fulminated but then a third voice was heard: Reason is a clever whore. It was Laufer.

Shaw looked at him and had some trouble getting him in focus. Then he straightened: sitting straight he was taller than Laufer standing. Oh yes he said You are the one who drives the East German car the Luthermobile. Ratty perked up at that. Oh yes said Shaw to the priest Of it it is said Here I stand I can do nothing else God help me. Ratty convulsed and Laufer did an imitation of a rapidly heated thermometer.

Marianne said Simon but they ignored him even Jan did.

The goddess of Reason said Laufer cutting off each word with a sharp knife Was enshrined by your sort in the 1790s in Notre Dame Cathedral: a common prostitute. Shaw yawned. Very appropriate I call it said Laufer: Ironically so. Ratty was momentarily undecided then joined the other Chaplain on that. That's true he said: It led to atrocities. Reason uninformed by Revelation always does. Shaw said to hell with them and stuffed his cat back into his pocket and rising bumped into Mrs Burger. She ignored him and focused on Laufer: Are you going to the movies or not?

He said he guessed he was. Was her husband along?

He'll meet us there she said and took his arm and led him off.

What's showing said Jan: Perhaps we could go too.

A Whodunit said Ratty: I saw it last night. So did Chaplain Laufer. It's pretty good. And by the way Lieutenant Simon I hope you'll come around and see me tomorrow about one of your men who wants to get married: an Airman Cholmondelay – pronounces it as it's written I believe.

He does? To whom?

What does it matter said Jan: That's not your business.

It is and it isn't said Ratty: The institution itself is what matters most but the Lieutenant is responsible to see that a grossly inappropriate match isn't made. So am I responsible. Her name is Moreau I think: Monique or some such Christian name. So you know her?

I've had correspondence from her: that's about all sir. Ratty nodded. He said he had to be going and for Simon to come around in the morning. As he got up to leave Shaw came back: I lost my cat he said I can't find my cat.

In your pocket said Ratty Look in your pocket. Then Ratty left.

Shaw searched but did not find. Must have fallen out he said. Simon asked him whether he ought to approve the marriage of Cholmondelay to a prostitute. Jan leaped up and glowered down at him: What!

Yes he said It's what she is. She was here tonight in fact with Longbow. He explained the circumstances. Jan was livid. Shaw was not: Sure he said Go ahead. It'll civilize the bastard. Her too. Always does. At least a little. Jan now was mad at the Professor too. Sure it does he said. A married man has to be responsible: gives him private property. People who own houses don't burn houses. Insurance premiums go down too: actuaries are notoriously unsentimental yet rates for young but married male drivers drop by half at least when they marry. You'll be able to do anything in the world you want to with him. Good idea Lieutenant: let him marry. He excused himself to search further for his cat.

Oh what filth Jan said making her hands into ineffective fists bent backward at the wrist and sure to break if she hit anyone really hard. His knees felt weak as he looked on them. Let's leave he said It's not too late for the movie. She looked at him with exasperation but cleared her face for Lieutenant Colonel Burger. He knew Jan from the hospital so had the right to ask her had she seen his wife.

Simon was about to say she'd gone to the movie but Jan stepped on his toes and said No. Burger nodded distractedly and looked around the Club.

Oh well he said. Then he thought of something: Your remarks at the Wing Staff meeting Simon weren't all bad. Good in fact. About planting trees. But they'll never do it. The Colonel said something though about your idea for a golf course and maybe a swimming pool was good. Said he liked it.

I never mentioned a pool or golf.

I know said Burger I know I know: but forget that and go ahead and plan it. It won't hurt you at all if you're thinking of staying in. He waved a hand at them and departed looking for his lost Rachel. They went out the front and he said they might as well walk over to where there was some open space and a copse of trees. He went there sometimes at lunch he said. But why had she lied about Mrs Burger?

He has enough grief poor man. It wouldn't do him any good and it's a shame what she's doing to the Chaplain. I didn't want him to know of it: maybe she'll be through with him and on to someone else and the Doctor won't even hear of it. It's one after another with her. She held his hand and swung his arm gently. The night was cloudy and making odd patterns against the moon as they moved along. He felt uneasy at the patterns.

I don't suppose it had anything to do with women protecting women.

It didn't: but it might as well have had. We find ourselves exploited by men. We have to do something to save ourselves. She wanted to know did he agree with Shaw about marriage.

Capitalism he said: Shaw was talking about Capitalism. Or at least Private Property. Over here he said I guess is where the golf course could go: start here and then stretch out along the flight line over there. He looked over to his left and said he guessed a pool could be worked in there but it wasn't really within his competence to build one. When he looked back Jan was running away from him. He caught her but she was crying furiously and hit at him ineffectively but sincerely with her fists. Damn you she said Damn you! He'd never seen anything like that and drew back: Reason he said she should be Reasonable.

I bleeve what I bleeve and you bleeve what you bleeve and we just don't agree she said at the eye of her storm. Then it blew past and the storm was on again and again she flailed and he let her go and she ran on. He walked back toward his BOQ but had gone only a few paces when someone bumped him and then rushed past waving something or other in the air.

It was Segal: he recognized the running style. Trousers were what he was carrying. Behind him he heard swearing in English by a voice familiar but for the moment not placeable. And Monique's French.

They were under the tree by the ditch where he took his lunch breaks. It seemed to him better not to go over there but to follow Segal back to the BOQ and see there what booted: it was growing on him that the voice was that of Bull Mousse and probably he wouldn't want to be seen sans pantalons by the likes of Simon. So he returned to his BOQ.

Segal knew nothing of it he said but only sat playing Charles Ives compositions on the tuba. He would say nothing and wouldn't even admit to being short of breath though such obviously was the case. So he gave up and as he closed door behind himself heard the first strong blasts of Aloob Aloob. Segal was slipping: he'd never before been unpatriotic.

Everything was in a state of chassis so he went outside and stood next to a small tree then looked up to count the stars and put Jan and everyone and everything else in perspective. It was clear and cold up there and nicely salted and he was calmed when three women walked past on the road. They were rapt in talk and looking at the other's face as women were wont to do. It was the nurses Blondie and Galway and someone else he didn't know and they either saw him not or else ignored him. Galway said she had news about O'Brien – Bridget from Pittsburgh? Oh sure said Blondie: Married a doctor. But he wasn't always one said Galway Not until after she put him through med school and do you know what he did then?

Blondie knew not.

Died said Galway. Blondie gasped and Galway nodded. *The dirty son of a bitch!*

XI

Grisby was upset: he did not have to get ready for the monthly parade as did Simon but Marianne was missing. We'd been intimate he said And I went into the latrine and when I came back she was gone. I was sure the door was locked and anyway I didn't hear anything. How in hell could it have happened? He sat down on his disheveled bed and palmed his face in his hands.

What time did it happen? I don't know: around 9 PM maybe. 2100.

Have you called the Air Police?

Grisby looked up at him to register his contempt and then put his chin on his fist: She's gone JP she's gone.

Well it's not as if you won't get her back. She can't have gone far. He looked at the wall behind Grisby where there was a travel poster for Spain. She could have gone there. Or to Scandinavia: that one was on the opposite wall. He would not mention those possibilities to Grisby. Well he said I have to put the Squadron through the paces for the parade. The only reason they have the fool things is to remind us that we're military. Guess that's a good enough reason if it helps discipline. He excused himself and put on the uniform of the day.

At Shaw's he saw things had gone as he'd expected: he'd lost a Bishop to Shaw's Bishop (stupid: Shaw should have moved his Pawn to Kt6) and with his Queen he'd taken Shaw's Bishop. At least Shaw had freed the QBP by moving it two paces forward which was smart since it kept it from getting fixed. Now he took that Pawn with one of his own. It was going according to plan: he was surprised Shaw couldn't see it coming.

He stopped by Jan's BOQ but she refused to open her door or else simply wasn't there. He couldn't recall whether she was on duty that weekend at the hospital. He would try again later. There was no way to ask the girl who shared the latrine adjoining her latrine to another room since being female she had extra privileges and both rooms were hers. So there was no one to ask after her the way someone could ask Grisby about him or he about Grisby.

On his desk was a note from the First Sergeant informing him that the Wing Headquarters Adjutant had called and unable himself to serve as OD that night had appointed Simon Officer of the Day in his place. On phoning the Adjutant he was told the man's wife had planned a special dinner party that evening and it had slipped his mind and as a bachelor surely Simon wouldn't mind. Simon would not mind he said but he was not feeling especially pro-feminine when he called on Ratty to assent to the marriage of Cholmondelay and Monique. Assuming Monique could be found.

She'll be found said Ratty And I suppose in due season you'll be marrying too although the only permission you'll need will be Nurse Gooley's? Well no he said he didn't think marriage was in the cards for him and Jan just then if ever: they had their differences. Religion for one thing. Ah said Ratty That's what you like about her.

Like about her?

Her assurances. Her certainties. Her Standards and Verities. He looked of a sudden very much like Barry Fitzgerald. You have none said Ratty And she has plenty: all she needs. And all her children will need too. But you have none. The difference is significant.

No he said It isn't like that at all. He saw another Sallman Christ over what must have been Laufer's desk in an adjoining office. Ratty had a cross with a barrel-chested Christ tacked over his. No he said Jan I like but not her Certainties which lack significance because they're based on ignorance.: my own Uncertainties are based on intelligence.

Ignorance! Ratty was on his feet and looked now like Pat O'Brien. Simon recalled somewhere that Barry Fitzgerald was a Northern Irishman and a Protestant. Ignorance! Tradition is what she has: you people have to do everything for yourselves or rediscover it. That's why you never get anywhere: all your lives or the better part of them you spend wondering what life means and by the time you decide you've found yourself or have the grace to call off the search it's too late to do anything with your lives. Except to talk about yourselves.

The talk sir is intelligent anyway.

Is it? Have you spent much time with Rachel Burger?

Have you sir?

Ratty remembered that he was a Major and pointed the way out for the Lieutenant. But he had parting words: Oh it would be wonderful wouldn't it Lieutenant if we were only intelligent apes who stumbled out of trees! Nothing would matter then: but your wishing it so I'm afraid won't make it so.

He was in a corner and decided it would have to be Laufer to whom he next applied for a Religious Retreat: these were good for five days in Berchtesgaden at a former Luftwaffe Rest Camp and you got two days to get there and two to get back. That was nine days Not Chargeable to Leave Time and they just about had to give it to you. Besides that he went to Church sometimes. He saluted and left.

The First Sergeant had the Squadron lined up and organized when he got there. But he wasn't quite ready to hand it over so Simon stood by the side of the road. Longbow was there. For purposes of the parade he would be the Adjutant: it would be his silly-ass job to walk quickly out from the ranks and salute the Colonel and tell him that all were Present and Accounted For. This he would do after receiving similarly formal and idiotic reports from the Squadron Commanders. Of which Simon was one.

Hey he said What happened last night Longbow with you and Monique and the Colonel? One minute you were with her then the Colonel was then Segal went bird-dogging after them. Longbow smiled and looked away: A little trouble there son a little trouble. Tell you about it presently. How you and Jan Gooley doing?

Not so good: religious trouble. He told Longbow what had happened and Longbow shook his head. You should never discuss religion with a woman See-mone: they take care of that anyway. And Jan don't care about your religion as long as she gets her way with the kids. What you in effect told her is that you ain't marriage material. You ain't ready for that yet: you just a jack-off. He left to take his place in the line of march and the First Sergeant told him the Squadron was ready. So he marched them along. He was to follow Base Supply Squadron and fall in on the apron behind them or rather alongside them. But they had moved on. No matter: he would catch them.

He liked marching and the rhythm of it: you could lose yourself in it and be free. And he was free: getting out from under Jan and the awful cloud of marriage. Private Property did indeed trap you and Marriage was indeed the Basic Form thereof. He swung along with the cadence and felt free.

As they turned along to the flight line he sought out the Base Supply Squadron he was to fall in along side of. Some squadrons were in place already and the guidon bearers were out in front of them at parade rest but he couldn't see the one for Base Supply. So he pulled his troops into the next available slot and sent the First Sergeant down to check on what was happening: was there still a slot open for him next to Base Supply (in which case he would take Headquarters Squadron down next to them) or had another squadron taken up the slack (in which case he would keep his troops where they were)? The First left to find out. Longbow he could see was out in front already and facing those who would receive the review.

In five minutes the First came back: another squadron had taken their place so they should stay where they were. OK he would do that. So he did. He reported when it was his turn to do so then when the music began he faced around and gave them Forward March then Right Turn and so on. The band played *The Thunderer* and they processed past the reviewing stand and then on back toward their barracks. It took about an hour in all.

They were almost off the flight line when he saw consternation about them. Several people not in the parade were looking at the horizon and pointing at something in the wet water-colored sky. He halted his squadron and looked too. It was a C-119 trying to do a barrel roll. *By the damndest it made it.* He gave the squadron At Ease so they could watch legally since they were going to anyway. It's Segal Goddamnit said someone in back of him It's Segal. The voice was Longbow's.

The plane was almost even with them then flying parallel to them over the landing strip when it rolled over and for a few hundred feet flew upside down at an altitude of three hundred or so feet before the boxcar part seemed to fall through the wings and plow along the remainder of the strip exploding all the while.

Well said Longbow He wanted to do with a 119 what no one else had done before.

The fire engines were rolling out and heading toward the flames but it wasn't any use and they couldn't even get close to the fire at first. So he got the squadron dressed up and marched them back to the barracks area and dismissed them. At the Club he joined at table Cosmo Longbow and a Negro officer named Trend Pumpkinseed who ordinarily would have been gone to Paris by then to roll around with the whores and who came back on Sunday to wash his car. He was the one who had mocked Laufer. They were talking about Segal.

Too bad about him said Simon.

He's still alive said Pumpkinseed.

Huh?

They confirmed it. It's a very forgiving aircraft said Longbow but it can't forgive everything. He stirred the thick soup he was cooling. Speaking of forgiving where were you an hour or so ago when you were supposed to have your squadron on the line? I almost turned around and said One Squadron Missing Sir.

He said he had fallen in where he was because the Supply Squadron didn't wait for him and others got in between them in the wrong order. He protested that he had sent a man up to check it out and he had acted on what apparently was the false report of that man. But what of Segal?

Still alive said Pumpkinseed: they got him over at the Base Hospital now working on him. Burger's doing what he can. Amazing thing is he's still alive. Burned. Everything broken. He shook his head and turned to his food.

Fantastic said Cosmo It's just like a real battle: troops formerly were taught to drill because that was useful for bringing them up to the front line (and keeping them there) and managing them. Now it's vestigial that we march at all but don't you see what happened to you Simon is what happens in real battles? I'm a student of military history and I know that's how it goes (although on a larger scale of course). Gettysburg for instance: where was Jeb? Delayed because Moseby gave him an erroneous report on routing to Pennsylvania. Amazing. Unbelievable.

Yeah said Longbow: Happen in the real thing people would write books about it and have debates and Round Tables and all that. You didn't realize what an important figure you were did you See-mone?

Or Pearl Harbor said Cosmo with Roosevelt deliberately withholding the information of the coming attack. Withholding it from field commanders. Or the ditch at Waterloo.

Simon said he didn't realize how pivotal he might have been in different circumstances. Then a song began on the juke about a George Bernard Shaw play. What was it? **Heartbreak House.** No this one was about a hotel. Not a bad song but now came the weird over him: now would Cosmo ask about the song then Pumpkinseed would answer and then would come Mrs Burger and Longbow would pick up his soup bowl.

Who's the singer Cosmo asked and Longbow shrugged and Pumpkinseed said it was someone new: he'd been overseas too long to know for sure and there she was wringing her hands. As Mrs Burger approached they all bent over their lunches but Longbow was the one she had a claim on and it was he she asked What Does it Mean? Longbow cringed at her accent.

She repeated herself even as he shook off his soup spoon. Then he rose and picked up the bowl and dumped it on her head. The bowl rode her like a halo and she vaguely resembled a religious picture as she stood with shoulders hunched forward and elbows pinched tightly against her waist with hands rotating outward therefrom. Her mouth was open but she said nothing.

Fantastic said Cosmo Fantastic. Longbow replaced his spoon on the table and left. Pumpkinseed swallowed a couple of bites then stuffed his mouth full said Umph and left. Cosmo resumed consideration of the bit about the misplaced squadron: It's rather like Waterloo he said Or Hitler's mistake at Dunkirk or Stuart at Gettysburg or the British Admiral who failed to support Cornwallis at Yorktown. He gestured with a fork the way British Generals do in films then cut his meat and put a bite in his mouth with his left hand and continued to talk while chewing: he and Segal had that in common. Mrs Burger may have been watching them but they avoided looking to see. It wasn't my fault you see he told Cosmo It was the Sergeant's or else whoever was in charge of the Base Supply Squadron. Cosmo said Hmmm Hmmm impatiently as people do who are about to correct you: Yes he said That's what Major Reno said (though in his case certainly it wasn't his fault) and Guederian and all the rest of them.

They heard a noise and saw Mrs Burger had turned from them and was walking out the front door with the soup bowl still on her head. What an ass said Cosmo.

Yeah he said And her front's not bad either.

Cosmo snorted.

I have to go see Chaplain Laufer before he takes off for wherever: want to put in for a religious retreat.

You?

Nine days not chargeable to leave time.

Not me said Cosmo: Infra dig.

At the Chaplain's offices happily Ratty was out and Laufer was in but there was consternation and as he stood outside the opened door he fathomed slowly that Walsingham the Chaplain's Assistant had witnessed a crime of some sort indeed a rape and had reported it to the Air Police and was being calmed down by Laufer. Walsingham felt guilty for not having actually tried to stop it but only for calling for help since when he got back where the act was happening they weren't there. Yet it was only a minute or so that he was gone. Cholmondelay was the villain. The girl had on a purple skirt. But how could a little man like Cholmondelay manage a big woman like that? Yes he was sure she was big.

So that was where Marianne went. He cleared his throat and their voices stopped and he stuck his head around the corner and made his request. Laufer was happy to endorse him for the Retreat. And did you hear about Lieutenant Segal? No he hadn't. I think God is helping him out said Laufer.

In that case who put him in? He regretted his words as soon as he said them: there went the retreat.

Laufer's eyes narrowed in appraisal: I see that you are a Calvinist. Dutch Reformed? Presbyterian? But Calvinist surely. You have a French name: Huguenot?

Huguenot he said and left. That was a close one. And he had got himself into it. Perhaps it was God who got him out.

Grisby when told of the probable fate of Marianne was concerned primarily that she not be traced to him. He was pretty sure he was safe unless someone found out who the clothes belonged to and who had given them to whom. But he doubted that. He did not want Marianne back: no longer pure.

You ought to be a Moslem Grisby: they have a rule like that. Something to the effect that a husband can't take back a raped wife. OK OK said Grisby who wanted from him an oath. Pledged to secrecy he went over to Shaw's: after Shaw had shunted his Queen to R4 he'd started a Pawn forward to QKt3 and Shaw had taken a Pawn with a Bishop. His Knight was advanced to Kt5 and Shaw had threatened it with a Pawn to R3 but he had to forget it when Simon moved his Queen to R7 and put Shaw in Check. Shaw took the only possible move (King to Bishop) and he checked him again with the Queen to R8 (a better move than Knight to K4). Now Shaw had moved his King to K2. He took a Pawn by moving his Queen to KtP.

At Headquarters he clocked in as Officer of the Day. Sergeant Leigh from Maintenance was NCOD. They remembered each other from the

Officers' Club bar where Leigh worked part time. Leigh had twelve years in and already was planning what to do when he retired.

I have some land in Iowa sir a good piece of property and there's an existing structure there I'm going to remodel: it's going to be a café with a bar in it built in the shape of a piano. And it'll have black seats and white seats because it takes both the white keys and the black keys to play The Star Spangled Banner. Leigh confirmed this with himself by a clicked tongue.

Oh?

You know: blacks and whites.

Keys?

Uh no sir: it won't be segregated is what I mean. Blacks and whites like black and white keys. It takes both to play the National Anthem.

He shook his head fuzzily.

It's a metaphor sir a metaphor: it means something else besides what it says.

Oh. He fingered the holster of the .45 and wondered whether he ought to shoot Leigh. No not unless he intended to kill himself also.

The afternoon receded while he read and he and Leigh took turns going to dinner. Nothing happened until 2100. Then came a call from Base Hospital that Segal Jacob Levenson First Lieutenant USAF had died and the OD was to put in motion the process of notification of kin. Then came a call to him as Commander of Headquarters Squadron informing him that Cholmondelay was being held by the APs for a General Court Martial with a charge of rape. He walked to the window where the stars were making their nightly rounds. He had read there were 10 to the 9th power of them in our galaxy and there were more galaxies than that sum even. But only 2000 stars were visible to the earth-bound naked eye at any one time. When I survey Thy handiwork O Lord he said aloud What is man that Thou art mindful of him?

Sir said Leigh pleasantly surprised Do you read Kahlil Gibran? Have you heard of him?

He said that he had not.

XII

Early in the morning he rose from the cot he'd slept on at headquarters and took the jeep out to the flight line after telling Leigh where he was going. Parts of the plane were still smoking though most of the scattered portions had been scraped together into a pile. A guard challenged him until he saw the OD armband then waved him on. He kicked a small piece of metal off the grass and onto the heap. But first it knocked over a flat piece of rotting wood just inside the grass line: a party of ants had been thereby disturbed and were frantically running about most of them with a pod of eggs held aloft in two legs. They were saving the future of their race and had serious work to do.

Hello dere Lootenant. Longbow was affecting his Cajun accent and was saluting him. Look around you See-mone: you be nostalgic bout all dis in some year ma fren.

He said he wouldn't. Longbow said he would. They walked around the wreckage kicking at parts of it. What'd he do? Steal the plane? Longbow nodded. They walked some more. Simon lit his pipe.

You know I been thinking about it See-mone: Segal he didn't do so bad. They walked some more. Segal he live free and he flew an din never had to land. He live free. Longbow nodded in agreement with himself.

Is there perhaps some way a person could live free and still not have to die doing it?

It was another high clear day of robin's egg blue and the early sun touched them pleasantly as they circled again the wreckage.

Monique said Longbow And Cholmondelay too: they're almost free. Oh they pretend now and then to be bourgeois but mainly they're good people.

He let it go and saluted Longbow and left to go relieve Leigh. Then when there was time he went to call on Cholmondelay. Did he want a lawyer? Surely he did? No said Cholmondelay he did not: he tapped his head just below the hairline but over the eyebrow. Since this was a space of no more than one inch it took some precision: There's my lawyer said Cholmondelay. OK he said and went back to Headquarters to be relieved as OD.

Under his door when he got there was a note from Laufer saying a place had been found for him at the very next religious retreat and that he could leave immediately provided no one superior to him objected. But Orders could not be cut till the next day. The Headquarters Adjutant whose place he'd taken as OD said he could go though.

So he left a note on the Morning Report Clerk's desk telling him to put him down appropriately on the accounting and to have Lt Hoop sign for him. He would try to go across Europe on a Daily Bulletin. He had heard that one could: all one needed was a document of some sort that people guarding borders could stamp. So he picked up one and left.

Grisby asked him the usual question about the girlfriend in Paris and said he would himself come in with him some weekend and take some pictures. Kind of at loose ends are you Gris? I mean with Marianne gone and all?

I put a lot of work into her JP a lot of work.

Maybe she'll turn up.

No: gone forever.

Make another one. You know: only better.

No there'll never be another one. He sat on the tautly made bed unslept in the night before.

All disappointed lovers feel that way he said stuffing T-shirts and shorts and socks into his bag: You'll get over it. Grisby who had followed him into his room said he wouldn't.

He decided to call on Jan Gooley before leaving for the train. And should he take the easel or no? Good camouflage but one thing more to haul. No. Well Gris I'm off. Grisby rising to return to his own room told him to take good care of the Frauleins and he promised he would. At Shaw's he noted the loss of a Knight and moving his Queen to take the Knight's Pawn again put Shaw in check.

Jan did not answer his knock so he wrote her a note and slipped it under her door. He would be back in a little over a week he said and would call on her then. Knock her up then the British would say.

Daily Bulletin tucked inside his coat he took the last bus of the day from La Beauce to Dam Pierre and on to Dreux where he could catch a train for Paris. He bought a first class ticket and a paperback copy of **Les Carnets du Major Thompson** and sat on his suitcase and waited outside. Some few stared at him after they saw what he was reading and in what language and seemed offended at his disruption of a stereotype. In the train compartment no one noticed or else pretended not to. It was nice to ride six to a room: probably the space was used less efficiently than in an open central-aisle American car but then that was Europe for you.

You were put in a smaller group a more manageable group and yet were not spoken to. In his own country it was the reverse where it was open and everyone talked to everyone and immediately was on a first name basis. But that was to keep you at arm's length since if everyone if on a first name basis where do you go from there? If everyone is your friend then no one is. American loneliness was the obverse of American friendliness.

In Paris he had to change stations and had the option of taking a connecting train in two hours or six. The latter had a better sleeper so he chose that. After checking the bags through he took the Metro to the Champs and wandered about. Presently he found himself at St. George the Fifth Church. Germans ran it in WW2. He went in. Why? He knew immediately: to find the girl who had mistaken his bed the last time he was in Paris. This was as likely a place as any and more likely than most. But a service was going on: Evensong or some such. With a homily. It was the same man. He talked of how things were back in New York and reassured them all that it wasn't so bad: he'd had trouble getting certain attentions he said Until they learned who I was.... Then after a Martini and Rossi at a café he took in an American movie. It was a funny thing about kids trying to take themselves seriously although really it was only an excuse for raucous music: *Rock Around the Clock.*

For a quick dinner he went to the Pam Pam. Longbow had said that meant Prostitute in Japanese and laughed at it. But they had quick meals and thus served a lot of Americans. When he was ordering a man nearby with a Stetson on his table and rimless glasses on his nose was saying he didn't want French coffee he wanted Amurican coffee. He ordered his own meal in French and the waiter did not make fun of him as they had the first time he tried it. Still it was such as the Stetson who had chased out the Germans.

He walked to the station since there was time for it. At the American Legion lost souls from surrounding bases looked out at the foreigners: Enlisted Men who had come to Paris but were afraid of it. Although he'd gone to an American movie himself and usually spent his time on the Right Bank. But the Right Bank was what came from having been poor: the Left Bank students were poor only for a time. Nouveaux Pauvres. Most came from affluent families and would step back into a similar life whenever they chose. What they were playing at had not for him been a game. He was too well dressed for them anyway and they ignored him as he ignored them.

At the train station one left as usual the mundane behind as the sense of being suspended from normal duties arrived with the trains. Trains were finished in the states except for hogs and cows and inanimates and for all he knew soon would be so in Yurp too. (He would send Jan a post card. Was it better to be free of her or no? His stomach said no but on boarding the train the rest of him and eventually his stomach too said yes.) It was a bit like boarding the military where your life was plotted for you large and small and you had a Mission and were part of a Plan: even so was it on a train where there was an announced Destiny and of course one followed laid-down tracks and schedules. Although it seemed rather inflated for someone whose main work was signing the Morning Report still there was the illusion. He settled into his Wagon Lit with **Major Thompson** and read till he went to sleep naked between the sheets.

Then he glanced out some miles east of Paris and thought he saw something impossible: a chateau that belonged not even on the Loire but was grotesque as if done by a French Mad Ludwig and yet there it sat. Then it was gone. When he awoke it was Bar-le-Duc. This was it: his destination where he got off where his regiment went into the line and he was late. He sat upright and realized he was wrong by forty years. Lying back he felt his body recall itself as he watched the scene outside the framed window: little was moving and it seemed a tableau painted by Lautrec filled with sick yellow and olive drab. It was the solid colors that made it seem so: the effect of night lighting. That and the sordid subject of ghastly lit scenes and people in a kind of waiting room for Hades and damned most certainly and living in a world of illusion and almost aware of their own delusion but not quite and to the undiscerning eye convinced they were living life to the hilt. A sickness ran the length of his spine and weakened the bones of both legs as he lay there and waited for the jerk and moan and sigh and gathering again as pervert fashion the cars each pulled slowly with their behinds the whole alimentary length along. Men must have died young there in the Great War or perhaps in 1870. If not then at those times then at some time past or at some time yet to come: and they doubtless went to it and would go to it as sleepily as had he just then. And then the train stopped.

When he looked again he saw long skirts on the few women in the station and saw in silence an officer who was not old enough for his rank shout something to a company of men in long French-grey overcoats who were armed with long rifles and bayonets of two or more wars ago. The officer he saw suddenly was Jake Segal if one made allowances for time and place and just as the men came to attention the train crashed its cars loudly and began to more. It was gone.

He left the shade up and watched the land turn flat then hilly now industrial now farming now canalled but everywhere asleep. As they approached Germany the land got cleaner and the atmosphere got more charged more electric. Once he saw a dog curb itself: the dog saw him watching and was embarrassed enough to turn his head before proceeding with his business.

At Frankfort in the morning he changed trains. Before boarding he had time for a quick snack which the Germans were as good at as Americans except the food was better in Germany. People were bustling and purposeful and clean. He sent Jan a color post card on which he noted his regret at not getting to see her before he left but asserting that he would surely find her on his return. He had a clear cold beer and on his way back from the latrine (a separate one for men only) passed a small bar where American music came from a juke. Something about a Green Door. It occurred to him that an entire generation of teenagers could date and conceive their children in their cars on Saturday night and marry before he returned and do it all to background music on their radios and he would not know the music that for them held the world together.

At Munchen there was a bus that took GIs to the religious retreat center and he caught that. The center had been built by the Nazis as a rest camp for the Luftwaffe and was well appointed. There would be a service that evening: he would go to that and then leave for Munchen and Wien and would not return. Or maybe stay a day or two to find out if it was likely that one could indeed skip out on the thing and the Chaplain's Office was so inefficient or so soft-hearted that nothing would come of it. His Daily Bulletin had been duly stamped at the German border and he supposed that if that was so then probably so was that other bit of intelligence.

The evening service was a general Protestant thing addressed To Whom it May or May Not Concern and out of boredom he began to read in a Bible racked on the back of a pew in front of him. He chance-opened it to Samuel and found it very bloody indeed. He flipped back to an earlier one and it got worse: entire towns were Dedicated to God by the Hebrews by which it became clear it was meant that every man boy woman child baby granny cat dog pig (especially pigs) chickens guineas cows and all were killed. The Chaplain did not speak of that though but rather of a girl born who grew to young womanhood and married and had children of her own and matured and turned old and at last died: the beauty and mystery of life.

On his way back to his digs he passed a Jewish chaplain in the corridor. The young Captain smiled at him as though he recognized a coreligionist. Simon smiled back and went on.

The next morning they were awakened by a system that played the US Army station: something called *Go Ape* was on. A generation could very well date and copulate and start a family on that tune and he wouldn't care at all. Then back to the chapel which smelled strange: it wasn't incense though he supposed Catholics and Orthodox used it from time to time for their services but was something like fresh straw. The odor of sanctity perhaps. Or clean hair. That afternoon there would be a trip to Berchtesgaden to the Eagle's Nest and he reserved a place. After that he would leave.

With another Lieutenant who had driven down from Spangdahlem in his own car he went into the town for lunch. Swede was what the other called himself and he looked well named although apparently too tall for the fighter pilot he was. It was a small restaurant and had good food and no other visible Americans. Swede had been at Spangdahlem for over a year and to show his affinity for the culture began to speak even shout in German. Scheiss he said Scheiss Scheiss. Swede looked around to see how he was doing and said Scheiss a few times more.

A good thing we've already ordered Simon said.

The Eagle's Nest was similar to a State Resort for families except the facilities were limited although the view was good. The fireplace mantle and walls of the main lounging room had been graffitied over by GIs. Mainly it was just names and places they were from and dates. So that was what it came to. If he'd been American Hitler could have been a high school art teacher. Maybe could have got a commission in the Guard.

Taller he might have turned out differently though he was fairly tall for a dictator. Most were short: Franco Napoleon Mussolini Stalin. Or maybe they only seemed small since they tried to claim so much more than a man ought. He was himself not tall but too tall for that. Tallish people clearly were too uncertain about too many things to be dictators. Or were too certain about them. A lot of tall ones worked for dictators though. All in all the Eagle's Nest at Berchtesgaden was a banal place.

Munchen was different: it was Bock beer time and there was a party going on at some hill or other the taxi took him to. About 3000 Krauts were in a large hall singing and eating and drinking and half again that number did the same thing outside. Overhead was a blimp in the shape of a Heubelein mug and all around were bands and singing and drinking. For once he felt he had come home. Not alien. He drank outside for awhile then inside but in both places eventually linked arms and swayed one way then the other in time to the music. No one seemed to notice he didn't sing the words or even speak any words.

Outside there was dancing of a sort that didn't require a lot of training and a girl beside him took his arm and led him out with the others to it. It was a sort of skip hop skip hop hop thing and then you turned around and did it over again: the beat was heavy and it was easy to follow so that you could slip into the pattern of it and didn't have to think about what you were doing but could just do it and let yourself be forgotten. That was what he had always found so hard to do and at last he was doing it.

THE WOLF'S SIDE OF THE LITTLE RED RIDING HOOD CONTROVERSY

It is widely recognized by writers but ignored by everyone else that much depends on Point of View. The Little Red Riding Hood story for instance invariably is told from the girl's angle. Invariably. Attorneys appointed to defend Mr Wolf might argue that Red was a Commie or that she and Mr Wolf had something going before she turned on him or that Granny and Mr Wolf had something going or that Cacciatore (the hunter) was involved with Granny or that Red made a pass at Mr Wolf. They would tell it from *his* Point of View.

They would *not* use Objective P-o-V since it belongs only in Theatre and Journalism (and doesn't exist there either since the author decides what is to be reported/censored). In **DreiGroschenOper** Kurt Weill made Mack the Knife a hero who asks What crime is it to rob a bank compared to the crime of founding a bank? Not something John Gay had in mind two centuries earlier. In **Jesus Christ Superstar** the authors claimed to write from no particular theological stance but only did so from the P-o-V of Judas: Their Jesus was a Jerk. To them their popular Romantic Sentiment was Objective. Journalists see as Fact what they are culturally and temperamentally inclined to see as Fact and they censor what they don't see or what they see but don't like.

The other three P-o-Vs equate with Father, Son, and Holy Ghost: Third Person, First Person, and Third Person, Ltd.

The advantage of the Third Person is that the reader knows all that is going on, but there is a disadvantage of a lack of Immediacy: it all tends to be distant. Like the Bible which may be called God's novel. After tearing up a false start where a quarreling character (Lilith) was wrongly running away with it He began again with two characters He made free and then told to obey. (A lesser novelist would opt for one or the other, but that would ruin the story by the Deity as Novelist.) Of course Adam and Eve wouldn't obey and He drowned out their progeny or burned them out or sent in new characters (prophets) to speak His mind to them. (Which spokesmen often as not were killed by the rebellious descendants of the first couple.) At last in desperation He got into it Himself and wound it up satisfactorily.

The advantage of First Person is Immediacy. Lots of it. The disadvantage is that nothing is known unless the narrator sees it, and there always is the problem of the Unreliable Narrator. Indeed *all* First Person narrators are unreliable. Even as with Autobiographers: we don't know all or even much about ourselves and what we do know often we don't tell. (Can one be *sure* Little Red spoke honestly of her relationship with my client Mr Wolf? That Granny did? That Cacciatore did?) Even Jesus said He didn't know all things to come on earth. Only the Father did.

A nice Middle Way sometimes is achieved by the Third Person Limited which affords the feeling of dispassionate reporting since it is Third Person but at the same time there comes a certain immediacy from its being delivered by one fellow only. If one wants to, this sort of reporting may be brought to us (as with the Holy Ghost) by several different speakers. Or one may mix-and-match by using a First Person Frame in which to paint a picture about Third Person reportage: **Lord Jim** say, or **Gatsby**. Suppose that were done by Mr Wolf about Red. Or Granny about Red. Or Cacciatore about Red. Or about all the others. Imagine *At a Gate*.

XIII

He rented a small car and drove about the city and then headed outward on a road he knew not where it would lead but the countryside was pleasant and flowerful. Eventually he turned North and headed for Dachau. After lunch at a clean restaurant he asked idly what there was locally to see. They told him.

It was a comparatively innocuous looking place and did not seem so efficient as he had heard. He was told originally it was intended for the improvement of German stock and was put to other uses because of the pressures of the war: Hitler was a Darwinist. Except for the stacks it was not dominated by any tall buildings but only by the usual military-style proliferation of small ones. There was no list of people killed there but he was told many were surely named Simon. The guide asked him if they were relatives and he said no it wasn't likely. Were any of them named Jude he asked the guide. The man looked blankly at him so he repeated himself and then wrote it out. The man nodded and said indeed they were.

A girl next to him spoke to the guide in the man's own tongue and explained the confusion although the man still did not see how one named Jude would not be Jewish. The girl was bright-eyed but a little scruffy: she had lived in her clothes some days. Was she American? No she told him German: I was born here. In America she would have been in college and probably a sorority sort except she at present wasn't clean enough for that. She wanted a ride to Munich. Was he going there?

There was just room in the car for the two of them but seemed to count herself amply provided for. Did she live with her parents?

No she said her parents had died at Dachau. He looked sideways at her and saw her features were somewhat Semitic.

Then how did she live? She answered by taking his hand and lightly tickling his palm. Oh. It was too bad about her parents.

Aunts and uncles too she said And cousins and grandparents and a bruzzer: all of zem.

How did you survive?

She wasn't sure: she'd worn the yellow star and had been spat on but had survived. She was contemptuous of others for not having done the same.

Is survival so much a matter of choice in such a situation?

She said it was: They could have fought back. He asked her what with since the Nazis had such a wonderful Gun Control Law but she shrugged it off.

She wore tight fitting trousers that were black with small purple flowers strewn here and there: what you'd get on the bargain table at left-over time. Her top was red and fit closely too. Everyone dies she said facing him: The thing is when not whether. She said Whezzer. She turned forward and rolled down her window to let the air whip her dark brown greasy hair. Of course how you die matters too she added But how you live matters more.

He asked again what they could have fought with and she ignored him. So he asked did she like the way she lived then? They passed under a banner of a fat young monk holding beer steins aloft against a yellow background and they were again in Munchen. She said she got by and perhaps in time she would marry an Ami.

Write a novel about your unusual life. How you survived the war 30 miles from Dachau.

She shook her head: there was little enough unusual about Dachau. The Communists at Katyn did the same thing and the Russian farmers what do you call them? Kulaks? Millions. Starved. Soviets murdered Ukrainians. And the British and Dresden and you too. Turks with Armenians. Hiroshima and Nagasaki. And the Japanese were so bad in China they embarrassed the Nazis. Six million Poles (half Jewish half not Jewish) 10 million Germans 20 million Russians so what? You know what is unusual about all that? About Dachau?

He had not decided between Organization and Mechanization when she answered herself: Nothing at all.

He said No Pearl Harbor no Hiroshima. But you could go to Israel.

Too hot she said: Turn here.

She took him to a dark restaurant where people sat in booths with phones in them and placed calls to one another. It was cloudy with smoke through which most of the patrons looked over- or under-weight and all of them over-age. They too had survived a thing or two and were having according to their lights a good time. Are we to get a booth? We're already paired off aren't we?

She answered by steering him to a back room where young Amis danced with their girls: We could not have gone in the front anyway she said.

Why not?

This is for us she said It is saved for people like us. It was a noisy place with people dancing to something called All Shook Up except not all the Amis were keeping time to it but were instead dancing close to their loves so that when the music broke they drew back erect. Apeneck Sweeney times thirty. But the food was hearty and plentiful and Sarah ate it quickly at first and then slowed down only slightly toward the end: her starvation was of the body not the mind. Once starved always hungry in an ill-mannered way? Perhaps a different kind of starvation was what made one Intellectual.

She had no opinion on what made one intellectual and suggested they dance. She wanted him to turn clockwise instead of the way the wind blew in America and the way dancing people turned there. Why the swastikas in the latrine at the orphanage were backwards scribbled? When they sat down again he wondered where the American Dachau would be though he did not know about Katyn.

The Soviets killed Polish officers who were prisoners of war there. But surely you have your Dachaus. You just don't know of them.

Perhaps they're yet to come. Dachau must once have been a lovely village. She said it still was. No he meant when that was all it was known for. Formerly. She shrugged.

Somewhere he said There is in America a pleasant town that some day may be our Dachau. Or Katyn.

But you have some now. Several. I am sure of it.

He knew of none. She shrugged again and called him Very American. You people are Ice Cream Eaters. You walk like bears on roller skates. Listen she said looking away suddenly distracted I need some money: I have to make a phone call and attend to some things. (Sings.) Let me have five dollars please and I will return to you your change in a few minutes OK? He said OK and gave her a bill and watched her depart without her pocketbook. Discreetly he checked it: it had in it a change of panties and a rolled up brassiere and a tricot and a hygiene kit and the usual trash. All she owned probably. He had just closed the top when she apologetically came back to get it.

He sat and watched the troops dance to something slower for them appropriately called Loving You. Then the waitress took away their plates and raised his empty glass before him and he nodded and she returned with another Löwenbräu. By the time he had finished that one and one more it was clear that she was not returning.

The air was good to get out into: sharp and wet with glistening streetcar wires and silver rails. It seemed the right climate for a smallish but technically advanced nation that wanted to conquer the world to have.

Then a pack of young men floated by in leather coats giggling and glancing back at him. Perhaps they grew up without fathers but so had he. They at least weren't going to start any wars. Not the spawn Hitler imagined from Lebensborn Camps.

He got his bag from the hotel and went to the Bahnhof and bought a ticket for Wien and sat in the waiting room. Their station was less of a Cathedral than the American version probably because it was post WW2 the old one having been destroyed by bombers. Still there was the air of expectation there. Such was not to be found at airports: you took off and saw nothing for the short while you were in the air and then you arrived so comparatively quickly that it hardly seemed you had gone any place. No expectation in that.

He did not get a bed on the train but instead sat up most of the night and smoked his pipe and watched the occasional lights come and go and gradually grow gray and then minty green. The two others in the compartment slept: one a middle-aged man with his mouth open and the other a tieless young Central European. Linz he missed but they stopped sharply at a small place that looked to be posing for a post card. The other two woke and looked sleepily out then dozed again. Steam rose from the outside and a few figures moved through it then it was again unpeopled. Like a stereoscope photo then it appeared to him in three dimensionality: instead of seeing depth only in regard to the one item focused on each item was posed instead in its own singularity. As if the air had been removed. Everything was seen as it never had seen itself even had it eyes.

Then it was gone and the town merely posing again. The train sighed and moaned and again they were moving.

In Wien he got a room and bathed and slept until afternoon when he saw the Ring and then an Art Museum. He was very rich indeed. That evening the Opera: The Magic Flute. He didn't know what was going on but he liked it. Afterwards to a place likely to have a zither player who would ease into The Third Man Theme at some moment during the evening. Which is just what happened. As he turned to note the old fellow smoothing away at the strings someone drew a second chair to his table and ordered himself wine in German: it was Cosmo.

He nodded and Cosmo returned it as if the meeting were planned but clandestine and not by chance. Here on business Cosmo?

If you count as business.

I'm the business? How did you find me?

Easily. You're wanted back at La Beauce.

Immediately? No said Cosmo they could leave the next morning.

What happened back at La Beauce?

Much: Chaplain Laufer is having an affair with Rachel Burger and Airman Cholmondelay is on trial for rape or soon will be and you are appointed to settle the affairs of Lieutenant Segal.

Indeed. But it needs no Intelligence Officer to come all the way from La Beauce to call me back for this.

Cosmo smirked: I see you've been reading your **Othello.**

He started then smiled at Cosmo. No said Cosmo They really do want you back to do the Segal thing: your time off for the uh he looked around him For the Religious Retreat is about up anyway I'd say. He agreed. Then Cosmo swallowed a large portion of wine as if to prepare to tell him Hard News: Also I suppose you ought to know that Jan Gooley is missing.

His stomach informed him he was not as free of her as he had imagined. He looked about at the tan plastered walls cracked to just short of the point of falling down and settled on a faded motto: *Liebe* was all that was readable. Damn. Where has she gone?

Cosmo looked at him with irises suddenly ringed with white. Where? How should I know? That's the whole point of being missing isn't it? That you don't know where the person is?

You found me. Easily you said.

Your trail was wide. But then of course you weren't trying to evade me. But really: a Daily Bulletin!

But what about Jan.

Thought you might know. Not that it was his job to bring such people back: that belonged to Office of Special Investigations. They may have her by now. The only motive they have to go on is she was seen arguing with Lieutenant Simon after leaving the Officers' Club so he had better be prepared on that one. What had he done with his day in Vienna?

Surprised you don't know: went to the Kunst Museum then to the Opera. And you?

Heard some Bach. Brandenburg. Concerti which came from one of the happiest periods in Bach's life the years from 1717 to 1723 when he was director of music at the court of Leopold of Anhalt-Coethen.

That so?

Yes. What we know today as the Brandenburg concerti turned up in a job lot of manuscripts sold in 1743 from the library of Christian Louis Margrave of Brandenburg on that ruler's death. Johann Sebastian Bach born Eisenbach Germany March 21 1685 died Leipzig July 28 1750. Concerti No.1 in F.

You memorize things easily.

Cosmo nodded: Can't help it. Fantastic ability I have: no way to suppress it. Helps in my work of course. Did Simon like music? Yes he said and tried to think of someone good he had heard and then he said Dvorak and then Cosmo told him it was not pronounced DeVorAk and said how it was pronounced properly. Unbelievable he said but Cosmo didn't hear it because someone was pulling over another chair and inviting himself down: An Army Major he said he was. Joined when he was fifteen. Got one more year to go.

You must have been in the big one Simon said and immediately noticed a small-size Medal of Honor on the tweed lapel. Yeh said the Major What do you boys do in the Army? They corrected him and he accepted their Air Force allegiance while rasping a thick-fingered hand over whiskers only a little shorter than his crew cut. Just back from Yugoslavia he said. Nice there: quiet music and everything moves slow. Found a nice girl.

That's hard to do Simon said. Cosmo said *she* probably found *him*: assigned to him by the government to spy on him. That so said the Major. He didn't care: so long as they were good in bed. He had a map of the world and every country he went to he always got him a girl. He looked around: Nothing much here. Might go out and have a look at the Hungarian refugees tomorrow. Might find something there: you claim to be able to help her get out to America or something. You boys fly?

Yes said Cosmo and LMDs said Simon: 3X5s. The Major admitted familiarity with the craft. Where were they stationed?

They told him and he shook his head about the Damned French: Best thing Ike ever did or ever will do was to keep us out of Nam: Never follow the French he said. He swore and said Every one of them thought of himself as an Intellectual or Artist or both.

Then he settled down: Were they staying in? No said Cosmo and yes said Simon. Cosmo was surprised but interrupted his amazement to order another glass. They all had one.

You're an Intellectual Cosmo said You won't be able to stand it.

That so asked the Major. He raised his eyebrows focusing piggish eyes upon him. Simon recalled that as animals went pigs were intelligent. Yes sir he said The worst thing to my mind is a wasted one. That means I better stay in. Cosmo was trying to clear his head. It makes sense Cosmo: I must some way get money. Otherwise my entire existence will be taken up with it. This way I'll be free by age thirty-five: Like the Major. Meanwhile I can continue to examine life: As someone said The Unexamined Life is Not Worth Living.

Cosmo promised to buy him a microscope.

The Major had discovered a female he'd not seen before who interested him. That may be he said But boys you will have to excuse me. He clapped Simon on the shoulder: Just because the unexamined life isn't worth living doesn't mean the examined one is. Don't expect too much. Excuse me.

Copulo Ergo Sum said Cosmo as he swirled his oily yellow wine: You might consider a long Axiological discussion with Rachel Burger when we get her back Simon.

She's off with Laufer I thought you said.

Patience he said raising a cautionary hand Patience: wait your turn.

You're well-educated Cosmo and don't know what it means to have no particular background: you've no idea how expensive ignorance is.

I may know it. But one thing Simon in your new-found life of questioning. Don't be like Rachel: wait for an answer. Or ask sensible questions: every Question contains its Answer one of my Profs taught me. If it's properly asked that is: the thing is not to ask Twaddle Questions. And do wait for Answers.

He said he would. Then came the Major over with a girl for each of them. The Major's had not come alone and she wanted company for her friends. Simon's was medium height and red-haired and she danced well enough except when she raised her arm an all too human flavor drifted from an exposed damp wad. She knew few Americans since there was no Base in Austria. But she knew all about America.

She did not like their racism she said: she would dance with a Negro she said. He commended her for that and she was bothered. Then after waiting a decent interval he asked whether she would dance with a Jew and then he found himself suddenly dancing alone. Cosmo nearby left his girl just as sharply with a command that she pop off or else that he must pop off or else he'd seen a Popov. Departing he told Simon they'd leave the next morning.

THE ERROR OF SOCRATES

Euthyphro is on his way to report his father for killing a slave his father had tied up while going to report that slave for killing another slave: the tied-up slave had died during his father's quest. Socrates (who is about to be put on trial for impiety) encounters Eurthyphro and questions the piety of the latter's action.

The thing is this: if one's father has killed (however inadvertently) a slave (even if it was done in the process of seeking to determine that slave's own guilt in a homicide) then one must either report one's father or one must not. Some sort of clear action is indicated. There is irony of course in the conflict of pieties: it is pious to punish murder but it is not pious to prosecute one's pater. Nonetheless *something* has to be done, even if it's wrong.

However instead of leading Euthyphro to some action or other what Socrates does is lead him to a position of befuddlement: what is piety? (What the Gods want.) Do all the Gods want it or only a few? (All.) Do the Gods themselves agree among themselves as to what is righteous? (Well....) Thus there is some conflict or lack of clarity. Also: what the Gods love is pious and that which is pious is what the Gods love. Not too much of a clarification there. What Socrates seems to dislike is humans providing for the Gods a service that does not improve Them (servitude) and also he dislikes the very *idea of Gods*.

So did others at the time: we have only a fragment of a penny tract sold in the marketplace of the day, which tract beings *Whether the Gods exist I do not know*. That is all we have of it but it is a lot since it says that ordinary folk could question this way with impunity. Others opposed Socrates: Sophocles wrote **Oedipus Rex** to assert that the Gods *do* know.

One pays one's nickel and one makes one's choice.

Socrates pled further at his trial for corrupting the young that if he did indeed corrupt the young then he still should not be punished for it since he would not knowingly create worse citizens of a society he had to live in and what one does unknowingly one is not responsible for. (Patently silly: everyone wants to Do Good: Mao sought to do good when his Great Leap Forward killed around twenty million people.) What Socrates claims anyway is not *ignorance* of the Law but *denial* of the Law. For that is what mainly is at issue: that there is a Law beyond the making of man.

He says in illumination of this point that he doesn't fear punishment of death because at death one of two things happen: that we enter an endless and dreamless sleep (a step up) or else our souls are freed of earthly bonds and go to a better sort of existence (a big step up). This he concludes because from mathematics he knows there are truths independent of earthly observation and he knows also that the senses lie to us (though it is by means of the senses that we know this). He is in short a Dualist: Matter and Spirit are separable and at death Spirit (which pre-existed before joining with a body) continues to exist. He knows this is true because his god tells him when he is in error. But his god is only a sort of logical check that tells him if the conclusion follows from the premise.

What he does not believe is that his premises might be wrong. Thus if Dualism is wrong then his conclusions are wrong: GIGO.

What Euthyphro is (however clumsily) is Theist. He says the Gods have Laws which we disregard at our peril. Or he would say it if he could. Maybe he did: it's easy enough to win an argument the day after. Especially if you're writing your own version of it in a dialogue. Or novel. It could be that Socrates lost every damned argument he ever was in and Plato wrote it down *his* way to make it come out better. It could be. Not likely, though.

Of course Socrates didn't have the uniquely Hebraic notion of a deity totally separate from His creation in which He interfered: that is, Theism. That left him one of the two Atheisms: Pantheism or Dualism. He was of the latter persuasion.

Whether Socrates deserved death for this corruption is another matter, though of course it is written that in War the First Casualty is Truth. And

Athens had lost a war. Someone had to be blamed and a former student of Socrates had been a turncoat. Corrupted. But by Socrates? Aristotle's most famous pupil was Alexander the Great. Is Aristotle to be blamed or praised because of him?

Certainly Societies function most smoothly (if stupidly) when no one asks *Why?* Intellectuals are like balky children in this regard. Except they're too smart for their own good. Thus they are unpleasant fellows and are as disliked as Minorities. Whom they resemble: Minorities just by being there question the Majority Status Quo. Minorities always have a different way of doing things and yet seem to function well enough. This bothers Most People since we don't generally enjoy being questioned on every blessed (You mean it's *not* blessed?) Act we choose: for one thing it means we but slowly get on with doing anything other than asking Why Why Why like a three-year-old who is no more listening for a reply than was Socrates.

The unexamined life is not worth living? Perhaps. But those who assume nothing can come in from Outside are like gerbils turning a rotary cage they can't escape. That is why Revelation is hated and even feared by Intellectuals. By definition it cannot be claimed by rational questers. So what Intellectuals examine are their own cages. Such examination may be worth doing but it is limited in scope.

Of course the Hebraic discovery may be a fabrication, an error; in that case, the mischief is theirs. But if correct, it gives a unique structure to the cosmos, one that has profound consequences.

XIV

Shepherds were feeding their flocks not far from where Simon took his non-lunch break. The course with Shaw was over and another had not yet started though there would be another one and he had no particular book to read so he had spent the morning studying the Uniform Code of Military Justice. Except for the time required to sign the Morning Report. The shepherds were on the other side of the Perimeter Road and fence next to a wheat field but the bleatings were clear enough. That afternoon there would be plenty to do: he was assigned to clean up and organize for shipping home the personal effects of Jake Segal. That could take some time depending on how much stuff Jake had.

The wheat field was thick and wild under a lowering sky of almost cobalt blue and crows raged over it: like a golden-haired man going out of his mind. It was all animate all of it: alive and electric. And next to the wheat field were the stupid sloe-eyed sheep. Back to work.

From the BOQ he rang the Orderly Room and told them not to expect him back that afternoon: he would be working on the Segal matter. The First Sergeant would call him if anything came up. The game with Shaw meanwhile was closing fast: after Shaw evacuated his King to Q3 he had moved his own King to K2 (a good move!) and Shaw moved his Queen's Rook to B. He then advanced his Rook to B4 and Shaw moved his King to B3. Next he moved his King's Rook to Q3 and to protect his King Shaw moved it to Kt3. This left Simon free to advance his Pawn to R4. The final stage had begun. But he had to see to Segal's last things.

His first job was to pick out a clean Class A uniform for burial. Surely it would be a closed coffin but they wanted the stuff anyway so he found what was required and put it aside for shipping to Orleans Depot where they still had the body. There was nothing of an embarrassing nature that the parents would be better off not seeing but every single item from a pocket comb on up had to be entered on a log. There was some money in a case in a drawer that he counted and entered on the list and more books than he knew any Air Force officer had and of course the tuba. Segal's bank account showed a modest savings and he owned a Kharman Ghia which Simon would see shipped back to survivors. It was all counted and duly listed and matched up by dinner time except for one pair of trousers that couldn't have been Jake's: too big. He set them aside and went for a quick bite at the Mess Hall.

It was while he was finishing off his cobbler that it occurred to him whose trousers they were and where he had seen them before. He went back to Segal's room and tore up the manifest on which the trousers were entered: there were only three items on the last page so he got a new sheet and re-entered just the other two. Those trousers might be useful to him and very soon so he took them to his own room for safe keeping. Then he was through counting up Segal's stuff and soon Segal officially would not exist anymore except to some Veterans' Affairs Office in Washington where the ripples of his life would perhaps be felt for fifty years. But as one who left no heirs probably he would be gone in thirty.

It was reward time so he went back to his room to stuff his pipe for a smoke. He resolved soon to give up the habit. He decided on a drink at the Club and knocked on Grisby's door to see if he was for it. He wasn't: he was reading alternatingly in a Sports magazine and in a Business weekly. No said Grisby Marianne had not turned up anywhere not had Jan Gooley though he had it by the grapevine that she was in no harm just resting at a French convent somewhere or other and it was all official. Simon told Grisby he hoped so.

Down the hall Shaw had advanced his rook to B2 and he moved his Pawn to R5. Surely Shaw must see it coming by then. At the Club there was at table no one he knew well enough to join so he took a stool at the bar and ordered a King Alfonso from Leigh who was just then telling a Captain how on a tour in Algeria he had learned to hate the French. It was a pleasant drink and settling and one that didn't lead on to more and more. Not that he had drunk too much since his intense concern and involvement with Jan had ended. Shaw was right: it was Sex plus Jealousy. Get rid of the Jealousy and you were OK. The brown and cream of his drink were just starting to moil intriguingly (like sex and jealousy maybe but he did not like symbolic thinking and rejected it) when he saw the mirrored eyes of Mrs Burger fixed on him above a doubled bottle to Old Swampcat. He looked around: Where's Laufer?

She put a solicitous arm on his and paralleled it down to his hand on which she warmly laid her own: Please she said That's over. She looked meaningfully at him and he had the sinking feeling that she had made her choice for Next. She had heard about his troubled Airman Cholmondelay.

He's not troubled he's just falsely accused. But I'll get him off. Leigh was listening while pretending not to.

Good she said we must help the sick. She had been to a Psychology Class and had learned about Sick People: we must help them he said.

He's not sick at all: Cholmondelay is charged with doing something bad that's all but he didn't do it so it's OK.

He's not bad she said still insisting on buying a horse he had told her he didn't own. Do you know what it means she said scarring his hand with her nails To be sick? To do something that is sick?

Yes said a super ugly Abraham Lincoln in back of them: Shaw's head formed the top point in a reflected isosceles triangle over their bottom or base points. Yes he said I have killed my cat. Does that make me sick? He rested his hands on the outer shoulder of each of them and was making himself steady thereby: he was hideously ashen-faced drunk.

Why asked Simon.

Shaw shrugged: because I am Sick I suppose. Isn't that what Sick means? When you do something so Bad no one else would do it?

How could you? Rachel Burger was aflame.

With my hands he said With my hands. He tried to raise them to show the scratches which now they plainly noted but he could not do that and remain standing so he left them settled where they were.

Thus pinioned they could only wait for a fourth party to bring relief. Sick? He said softly to himself: Am I sick? He was getting whiter by the moment and at the edges green. Sergeant Leigh was wiping his hands and making ready to come around the counter where the gate was at the far end. The little feline would not stop drinking so I throttled her that's all. Sick? Shaw's hands were leaden and Rachel Burger was being crushed from his power without and being burned by her rage within when a small bare arm showed around Shaw's waist. Then a second snaked around from the other side and his hands lightened then drifted off. Turning Simon saw it was Queenie Compson: she was managing him beautifully steering a bull around china or a ship past ice floes as she got him away from one white-topped table to another without hitting any.

Leigh came back behind the bar and resumed his washing of glasses: I guess she's been in that condition so much herself she knows how to handle it.

She's a refugee Rachel Burger said: She came here from Germany. Not just from Rhein/Main but from Germany where she was interned during the war. She was visiting her mother and got caught there. That's why she drinks: she's a refugee.

Sergeant Leigh began wiping in front of them: You never drink he said: You never drink Mrs. Burger.

She began to consider Leigh with seriousness.

I'm not a refugee she said to Leigh I'm Jewish. Did you know that? He did not know that. Well I am she said And there is no word for refugee in Hebrew.

A voice discreetly in Simon's ear had it that such went a long way toward explaining the plight of the Palestinians. It was Chaplain Ratty and he was tugging him over to a table. Simon turned to excuse himself to Mrs Burger but it was not necessary. She had indeed noticed Leigh.

They found a table amid the confusion of the band striking up In Munchen Steht Ein Hofbrau Haus with the predictable chorus following hard on and Pumpkinseed and an officer he didn't know greeting each other after a separation: Pumpkinseed's words had mainly to do with the gastro-intestinal area with some attention given to the genitals while this friend spoke lightly of the Father and the Son. Ratty's face clouded.

Why that Lieutenant wants to talk that way I don't know.

Pumpkinseed?

No the other one. Sordid. He looked about as might a spy for God. It was at least sordid he sighed and then opined that if the deity could stand it he supposed he could too. He wanted to talk about Cholmondelay: what was he going to do about Cholmondelay?

Get him off if I can. And I think I can.

Ratty had not looked for that and began to seethe then he settled back: Yes of course you would. What will be your defense? That he didn't get enough ice cream when he was six years old?

No sir that he didn't do it.

Are you sure of that? Well yes he said he had looked into it and was sure Cholmondelay was ridiculously innocent. Ratty said he also had looked into the matter and was sure the man was guilty.

Well sir that's why we have trials he said And Courts of Law and all that: so an innocent can't be got.

Innocent! Ratty said he knew his type well enough: Your type shouldn't hold commissions. It's too hard for you too hard to be an Officer: then you can't just tear down and act smart you have to hold things together. Unfortunately our society makes a virtue of dissimulation not integrity. Defender of the Underdog indeed: very Romantic. Ratty removed the brassiere and then the panties from his Beck's then played his ace: I suppose you wouldn't think it a matter of any great concern if the girl he raped is pregnant?

He sat hard on his cushion as if his laughter would come out that end if he didn't. He said it would indeed be a miracle. How was that asked Ratty. Simon couldn't say.

Ratty was adamant: I say punish the man. St. Thomas says castration is appropriate in such crimes. Moslems do it too. Or are supposed to. Or death.

And deprive the bastard of his father? Surely you don't recommend abortion?

No Ratty did not as it was not after all the child's fault: as an orphan did he not agree? As an orphan he couldn't say but he excused himself and went to the stockade to see Cholmondelay. They were allowed to speak privately and at length. Clearly the fellow had no mind at all but through bits and patches of what he said Simon was able to piece together the puzzle: he had seen Simon with Nurse Gooley at the Hospital and then thought he Simon had taken Monique to the Officers' Club and he got drunk and got revenge by jumping the Nurse. And where had Cholmondelay found Nurse Gooley? In the BOQ he said which he took her out of but he was drunk and could not recall precisely the details. He kept a blade to her throat and she didn't say a word.

I'll bet she didn't.

That little twit Walsingham saw them but that was all.

He did not bother to correct Cholmondelay on the matter of Monique about how it would have been Longbow and not he: it didn't matter. You're innocent he said And I can get you off.

Because I was drunk huh? His small dark eyes glowed dimly: a loophole.

No he said because you are innocent: you'll be out of here in a few days. I guarantee it. Cholmondelay's eyes again grew dull but he said he guessed the Lieutenant knew what he was talking about.

Back at the BOQ he got out Segal's extra pair of trousers and checked them again. The only other thing odd about them (besides their being too big) he now was able to place: they were stretched slightly on the right side of the fork or at least were shaped so that if worn that was where the goodies went. He would call on Colonel Mousse in the morning.

He wrapped the trousers carefully in a neat package and put them in the back of his closet: he would not put it past the Colonel to have his room searched and get the trousers back that way. So he arranged the liquor bottles on top of them in a manner than made it very unlikely they'd be found. Then he opened a bottle of Cherry Heering he'd bought mainly for the color and poured himself a cordial. Slowly he drank it and smoked his pipe and read in the works of Claude Henri de Rouvroy. He was living the good life.

Or he was until he heard Laufer and Shaw arguing in the hall whereupon he put away his book. When they went into Laufer's room he entered Shaw's and saw the professor had moved his King's Rook to QB. So Shaw saw it coming but too late. He advanced his own Pawn to R6. That done he slipped out and walked to the Club. And there blowing noisily at the bar was Colonel Mousse.

He approached boldly and stood waiting to be recognized. Probably Mousse would hear his heart pounding and turning would see his shirt rising and settling in quick agitation as Simon was sure it must be doing. He looked down: it wasn't. It was with his head thus bent that the Colonel addressed him: Well what's your excuse for living?

To clear Airman Cholmondelay of false charges he said.

The Colonel grew dark and then on hearing about the trousers grew darker yet. Follow me he said and strode quickly toward the front door but turned abruptly before he got there and went into the Men's letting the door swing back at Simon. Mousse checked the stalls then went up to one of the urinals and stood there and indicated that Simon was to do the same at the adjacent one. The son of a bitch is guilty said Mousse And I want him in Leavenworth for twenty years: now bring me back my goddamn pants or wear them yourself or send them to my wife with a note explaining everything I don't care which. He hauled out the while his willie but Simon noticed he wasn't using it: a bluff then.

No sir he's innocent and I can prove it in court but it would be simpler (and less embarrassing) if it didn't go that far: he was arrested on the Chaplain's Assistant's word and not on the woman's and the woman hasn't made a charge and I can assure you she won't.

Mousse wanted to know why she wouldn't. He started to tell the Colonel that she couldn't but then that would lead to one thing and then another but Mousse insisted. So he told him.

Mousse was stone silent for some seconds and then began to laugh so loudly he thought everyone in the Club even those around the piano would hear. Then the Colonel began to relieve himself and the crisis was over.

OK he said I'll transfer whatisname tomorrow. What is his name? Walsingham sir. OK: Walsingham goes to Thule. Or Daharan. And the charges will be dropped you have my word. He extended a hand for a shake and Simon hesitatingly took it after considering what else it had just shaken. Then back to his BOQ.

Laufer and Shaw were quiet then or else had gone away and the hallway hung empty: the floor and the sides and the ceiling proceeded toward a vanishing point beyond the opposite doorway into black night. Inside where he was it was noiseless and like a tunnel with the walls turning concavely away from him and the ceiling too and walking on the floor was like trying to get through the rolling barrel at the Fun House.

Yet he was not drunk. He tried to lean on one of the slippery walls and instead found himself on his side on the floor: but he retained his sense of direction and snake-like made his way to the room past Segal's now empty one and Hoop's and Laufer's rooms both quiet and on the other side Grisby's not silent: there was rustling going on inside and fussing and murmuring. It was unmistakable: BM had found Marianne somewhere or other and had returned her to her rightful place in his bed.

On hands and knees he got to Shaw's where behind a partially closed door the professor lay drunkenly snoring. At the sight of the game board the vertigo left him and he saw it had gone as expected: Shaw had moved his Bishop to Q3 no doubt to gain as much as he could from the coming loss. He took Shaw's Queen with his own and put him again in check. Only temporarily and he would lose his Queen but surely Shaw saw that Mene Mene was written on the wall.

Thence back to his room. Next door was Grisby with Marianne in bed. Yet Grisby had sworn he would never do that since she doubtless had been with another man during her absence. No convent rest for her! Ah but absence makes the heart grow fonder. Brilliant saying: Out of Sight Out of Mind. Those quips were always counter-balanced. Just like philosophical positions. And it was well that it was so: he felt both ways about Jan Gooley and both quips fit. Again came the vertigo and he slumped. The quips fit but his key didn't: with his other hand he pulled himself up by the door knob and then the key went in and the door slid open and he rolled past it and in. He got it closed and sat with his back against it and gradually the walls became vertical and the ceiling and floor became parallel to each other and perpendicular to the walls and all was well. Slowly he got up and cautiously moved toward his metal desk but caution was not needed: he was fine.

Then he saw that the bathroom door was open and he went closer to hear what Grisby was doing. He bent his ear to the far door and concluded that matters were coming to a crisis. Then after a pause he heard Grisby talking softly and then there was a similar female voice: the joker was doing an imitation of a woman. But not with a French accent. And not terribly authentic.

Then at once feet hit the floor: he hadn't time to get back in his own room so he slipped behind the curtain into the shower. Immediately Grisby's door opened and the toilet seat came down. Aha! Shouted Simon leaping from behind the curtain to confront Grisby but stared instead at Jan Gooley who had been just starting to pee and suddenly was in near shock as she sat naked on the pot.

XV

He went to the second showing of the movie to get out of the BOQ and away from Grisby and Jan: Grisby was angry he'd seen her naked and she was angry he'd caught them and as for himself he felt eviscerated. No more no less. He didn't feel anything at all in fact: a gutted fish didn't suffer any longer did it? Flopping around on the bank sure but not once it was cleaned and he was as clean as they come. He almost floated to his seat. As luck would have it the seat was next to Laufer although he did not at first realize it. Probably because the Chaplain had his civvie jacket collar turned up and his head scrunched down and was sitting on his kidneys next to the wall.

He looked in fact like a derelict sleeping through a double feature two or three times but the theatre was full and there wasn't another seat. The film was a vehicle for a singer Simon didn't know but who had become popular since he'd left the States. It wasn't till the recording of Love Letters in the Sand went off and the lights dimmed that Laufer rose up a bit and was recognized. Well he had his troubles too and the Chaplain's were also female. They nodded to each other and began to watch.

By the time fifteen minutes had passed Simon doubted he could endure much more whether Jan was in the sack with Grisby or not: in the midst of the Luzana boonies was a cabin in which the hero resided and there he heard approaching hoof beats. Running to the window to look he quickly returned and announced that Someone Was Coming. Simon leaned over to Laufer and said And Someone Else is Going. The Chaplain looked up at him and made a similar decision.

Outside they both realized they had nowhere to go. He told Laufer of his troubles and the man nodded and nodded: They don't play by our rules women don't he said Although they do play by rules. It's just that we're trying to Play the Game by Different Rules.

What was the difference?

Oh he didn't know: maybe they were each in it for themselves and they would turn on each other — women would — whereas men held to a more abstract pattern of rules but he wasn't sure about it. My experience is limited he said. They began to walk the Perimeter Road and presently began to pass the lined up 119s of one of the Flying Squadrons. The world of those who fly is a different world from ours he said but the Chaplain disagreed. No he said It only seems so: they have to land too. For a time they can delude themselves that's all.

Maybe. Who're you hiding from? Mrs. Burger? LC Burger?

Huh? Oh. Her. I mean no not her. Or him: I don't think he knows about it. She's had quite a few you know. For her each new man is like a new idea: this is the One this is it At Last *the* One and there'll never be another one and the last one didn't count or any of the others and there'll never be any more just this one. She's run off with Sergeant Leigh. (Soon to be Airman Leigh.) Not just consorting. Run off.

He stopped short: An Enlisted Man? Laufer nodded. Wow he said That'll be her ass. Laufer shrugged: Maybe. Oh it will be he said It will be: that's the unpardonable sin. She'll get sent home. Laufer again shrugged.

I'm hiding from Shaw he said.

Can't take the Positivism eh?

Laufer looked at him strangely and then took him by his lapels and stopped him and stood too close for anyone except Arabs and homosexuals and apparently Christians. You mean you haven't heard the Good News he asked?

Good news?

Christ Jesus is Raised from the Dead he said with eyes afire: Your friend Shaw has converted. He released his lapels and turned away and began walking again: Follows me everywhere. Zeal of the Convert I think they call it: never lets up. He's bought himself a Bible and he's already underlining passages a second time.

Good grief. He kicked a rock off the Perimeter Road and over the fence to where some sheep were standing looking stupid. They all hopped back when the rock fell then slowly moved up again to the fence. But he said You must be overjoyed: a stray returned to the fold and all that. What is it? More joy in heaven over one lost who has returned?

Knock off that crap. Laufer kicked a rock. I've been bothered for some time he said. You probably knew it. All bound up. Sitting on the pot the other night I said the hell with it. And I was free: constipation worries over. I have been a Fool he said but no more.

But what about your work?

He got a devilish look on his face: I'll get a job in industry. Go into an Executive Training Program. I know pretty well how the psyche works. I can exploit hell out of it: make a mint. He was thinking of the thick carpets and the good pictures and soft music and an all around New Life. He chuckled demoniacally. As an afterthought he added that he had resigned his commission effective in a month or so. He'd take a leave between now and then and see a few things (another chuckle) and have a few good meals and take in a flesh pot or two. Maybe he'd go to Lebanon or Tel Aviv. In the meantime the thing was to stay away from Shaw and he advised Simon to do the same: he had been a prize pupil of the prof's hadn't he? Yes? Then better stay away.

Well I'll be damned. So it's all up with you: no more horse race films. Or detective stories: whodunits.

I guess: it's more like a chess game anyway than a horse race. The Adversary has a few moves left but he has lost the game. It's just being played out in a sort of delaying action. Or so runs the story. I'm not very interested in the story now anyway. He looked at his watch and said it might be time for them to go back: probably Shaw would be abed then or at least deep in study. He had thought Hoop was something but that was before he met Shaw – Shaw as a Convert.

And before you met Rachel Burger.

Laufer broke stride only briefly as he considered it and then said he guessed so and chunked a small rock at the stars. The sky was wildly salted with them as if the Morton's girl had passed that way. Again the stupid sheep watched them while the two re-made their way down the moonlit asphalt to their BOQ.

When they got there they found it was safe after all: Shaw was still up but it was Hoop he had buttonholed. A fairly even match said Laufer as they slipped past. He told the Chaplain it was too bad Segal wasn't there to play them a hymn on his tuba. Laufer looked furtively back at Hoop's door before slipping to his own and whispering See You Around as he disappeared.

He went quietly as he could to Shaw's where he saw his Queen was indeed lost to the King. He took a Shaw Rook with one of his own. Then he returned to his own room and locked the door behind him. Grisby had locked the latrine door but of course his own key undid it and softly he made his way to the toilet. He most gently locked Grisby's door (which also could be unlocked but which would take time) and pondered whether to urinate in the sink or pot: the first would make noise when he rinsed it down and the second when he flushed. Because the bowl was next to their door (*their* door if she was still resident) he chose to sit rather than stand: by aiming at the ceramic he was able to be very quiet indeed. He leaned forward and listened: she was still there and they were at it again.

He flushed noisily and went to bed.

Next morning BM Grisby was up and gone before he gingerly knocked on the door to see if Jan had stayed over. If she had she was gone too. Nor did he see him at the Mess Hall. Jan of course ate at the Hospital. Odd that one so cautious in every way before about her reputation and virtuous in her ways suddenly should throw it all aside. He would have to puzzle that one out.

At the office there was a note on his desk instructing him to go immediately to see Colonel Mousse which he did. The Colonel's secretary smiled and nodded him into her boss's office and there was Bull Mousse himself lounged behind his desk with his feet up on it and most of him not visible behind cigar smoke. Cholmondelay was standing holding a gift cigar like a bashful piccolo player not knowing whether to begin or no. When Mousse saw Simon he gave him a cigar too: Light up he said to Cholmondelay Light up. You save yours he said quietly to Simon and held out a flaming lighter to the Airman. Cholmondelay lit up and stood looking like any other rat smoking a cigar. Stick with me Cholmondelay said the Colonel And you'll be farting through silk: yes indeed. Dismissed. But not you Lieutenant.

The Colonel looked over Simon's shoulder from his sitting position and putting his feet on the floor: he was following Cholmondelay's regress and Simon moved aside to allow better viewing and turned himself just as there was an explosion. Cholmondelay reappeared in the doorway with the shards of a cigar between his teeth and an approximate blackface around it: he had closed his yes apparently just in time so the area around them was lighter than the rest and there was a halo around his mouth. He stood there blinking like Mr Bones. Mousse meanwhile was laughing so hard he couldn't make noise. He waved Cholmondelay on his way and then when he got his breath back told Simon he too could go but if ever he found Marianne again certainly he would appreciate an introduction. He too was waved out. No salute: Mousse was too broken up.

Otherwise it was a calm day except when Shaw cornered him after dinner and asked him was he Saved?

Saved?

Yes saved said Shaw Are you Born Again?

Born again?

Born Again by the Grace of God!

Grace?

God is not mocked! Shaw thundered God is not mocked!

He decided not to ask *God?* But he said he wasn't mocking he just didn't know what those words meant.

Sin said Shaw There is the living proof of the depth of your sin: you don't even know what those words mean!

Sin?

Shaw's nose began to purple but then he saw Hoop ambling along as if following an invisible mule and plow and he left Simon for someone more simpatico.

Illigitimus Non Carborundum said Longbow suddenly at his back: You seen Brother Hoop?

Yes he had he said: right over there. But Shaw had found him first. Longbow said Hoop was approved for a return to flying since in the opinion of the learned physicians his Nervous Disorder was sufficiently settled that he could stand the stresses and strains of piloting. So said the learned physicians but Longbow clearly had his doubts. Behind him was the mural of the aircraft of WW2 in which conflict those there assembled had not flown. It cut Longbow that he was far too young for it though he'd not spoken of it. You want to do that too See-mone he said: Get back on flying status. Just because you can't cross your eyes and you passed out once don't mean you crazy like Hoop.

Who approved him? Burger?

Initially. They sent to Wiesbaden after that and the doctors there said with certain modifications he would be acceptable. Shaw bother you much? He gestured over to where the Professor was skull to skull with Hoop (whose head anyway with its taut-stretched skin looked like a skull).

Just of late: he asked me about sin or something. Really I've no idea what the word means. If it means anything at all.

It means not doing what you want to do. He sighed deeply and said right then he had to do something sinful: he had to go speak to Hoop and he didn't want to. See you later See-mone.

He went back to his BOQ and smoked and read awhile: it was an off night for class and he'd seen as much of the movie then showing as he could stand and at the Club they were playing Bingo. He read an essay on anti-Semitism in which Sartre blamed it all on the Middle Class Mentality and absolved the Workers. That was for his new Social Sciences class and for collateral reading he began a book on Authoritarianism which said the Fascist personality was fostered by sexual repression. It was multi-authored and some hundreds of pages long and he began skimming but largely that was what it said. He listened at Grisby's door but no one was there: well at least Grisby was not likely to go Fascist. But no it was not necessarily so: the Social Science he was reading was the sort of Science that told you why something had happened after it happened but was not the sort of Science that predicted with accuracy what *would* happen. It was not after all Mathematics or Natural Science. So Grisby was not yet off the hook.

Then there was a soft rap at his door. It couldn't be Shaw since he knocked many times and loudly so he was safe from that. On opening it he found it was indeed Shaw: even his knock had been converted. With the door opened there entered also the sound of someone's record player from an open door across the hall: whoever had taken Segal's old room was listening to something called Splish Splash I Was Taking a Bash and was making everyone else listen to it too. What a descent from Segal. Shaw meanwhile was standing there weaving slightly not saying a word but only evincing himself as a something less than seven-foot presence.

My God he said You're drunk!

Shaw glowered and brushing him aside entered. At least with the door closed Splith Splath was diminished. He could not think when stuff like that obtruded: probably why the nameless idiot played it. He had seen the fellow: young man new-looking and knowing him as newcomers did but Simon had not known the boy's name. Shaw seated himself occupying one and a half times over the second chair allowed each room. He looked at the book on authoritarian personalities: there was a time he said (and not very long past) when he would have been interested in such. Indeed his last publication had to do with Fascism: Will France Go Fascist?

That must have been written a long while ago. In the 1930s say.

No: a year ago. Or was it two? Anyway if you're interested I said they might. As likely as anyone: they're not particularly racist (except for Arabs) so theirs would be Cultural Fascism. He threw the book on the bed where it bounced nicely: his Tactical Officer from Air Cadets would be pleased except of course a bonne had made it.

I am not drunk he said Although you are not the first in recorded history to confuse my condition with that of the inebriate. He shook back his thick hair and tried to lean on the headrest of the chair but there simply wasn't enough chair. He jack-knifed forward instead letting his hands hang between spread knees. He was having a hard time getting it out. Finally he said You were my best student and I think I have influenced you some. Yes?

Simon felt like anyone else confronted by a large fellow one owed respect: Yes.

OK: I owe you – I owe you – I owe shall we say a certain amount of rectification. But I am having difficulty in knowing where to begin: I do not know at what point I cross wires with you and thus at what point those wires begin to grid and mesh. That is I do not know. I was drunk then and now I am sober. But you are still drunk.

No I am not drunk. I haven't that problem. How it hell would he get out of this? Oh for Segal and his tuba! Problem said Shaw with brows raised. Yes he answered himself: That's what it's called isn't it? A Drinking Problem?

Ah he smiled broadly: A Problem. You know what is nice about problems Simon? They imply a solution. Like Social Problems: such a statement tells us that if we arrange things properly socially there will be no more problems. The error in such thinking is that the problem may not be social. Also if one says Problem one implies Solution which for some Obsessive Personalities could mean a Final Solution. We know what that can lead to. Anyway leave problems to mathematics and speak instead of situations or conditions.

Good: now what I had is what is called a Sickness. But curiously it is not biological. Not in my case. Probably not totally so in others. It is a fault not of the Body but of the Will. It is only because it is so hard to overcome that we call it a disease: it is not communicable nor is it an infection of any sort. He paused and it occurred to them both that at this juncture ordinarily he would have a drink. Shaw laughed.

We say this he said summing up Because we do not believe in freedom: because we do not believe there is a true choice between Good and Evil but only between Correct and Incorrect. Which often is proper thinking but not always: Sometimes it is a question of not thinking correctly which leads to Error. But it is not proper when we say the maker of an obviously horrendous moral choice is not Sinful but is Sick.

If you call people Sick because you dislike their thought and acts then you in calling people Sick when truly they are Bad then you deny us our freedom. We are Free to Be Evil though the more we choose it the less free we are each succeeding time to choose but because we are free to choose Evil we are free to be human. Although as I said if we choose often the Bad then we do lose each succeeding time part of our future Freedom to Choose. Perhaps that is indeed a sort of Sickness of the Will: an atrophy. Only a jolt can bring us out of that if anything can. An awareness that our debt has been paid. That our habit is not necessary. That jolting discovery alone. But we are Free: make no mistake about that. External events impinge (and internal ones too) but wherever we find ourselves we may nonetheless choose.

So he said and slapping his knees got up: I have cleared myself of responsibility to you for past sins. Now you are on your own. But remember that I was saying a parable. He stood laughing at himself: Zeal of the Convert eh?

Then he was gone.

Simon followed after: did he not wish to finish the game? Shaw regarded him blankly. The chess game he said to the professor and Shaw said Oh so you are the one I have been playing: I thought it was my old classmate Mousse.

Classmate?

At the USMA (West Point to the vulgar): I went there you know. Wasn't so tall when I enrolled. Resigned my Commission. Couldn't stand it. Back in for WW2 and spent it all in Alaska. Worst experience of my life. But I did learn to play chess at West Point (all Cadets had to in those days) so I assumed it was Mousse. Well well. He looked at the board: Do I take your Rook with my Bishop or my Rook?

If you take it with the Bishop I'll move my remaining rook to B6 and it's over.

It's over anyway: I don't care any more.

You can delay.

OK said Shaw and took it with his Rook. Simon took Shaw's Rook with his own and Shaw with his Bishop took that Rook. Now what?

I'll move my Pawn to B4. Shaw moved his Bishop to Q and suggested they allow a minute a move: he wanted it all over. Simon agreed and advanced his Pawn to Kt4. Shaw sent his Bishop to B3 and when Simon moved his Pawn to Kt5 Shaw retreated his Bishop to R. Simon moved his Pawn to K4 and Shaw sent his King to K3. Pawn to B5 led to an exchange. Shaw sent his King to B4 and saw a Pawn go to Kt6 and there followed another Pawn swap. There was nothing Shaw could do after that to prevent defeat: one of Simon's Pawns at least would make Queen and Shaw would lose his Bishop. He resigned: It makes a nice analogue he said.

Indeed it did though he did not tell Shaw that: he had expected the professor to move his Pawn to King's Bishop Four back when he had moved his Rook to Bishop Two instead. Although it would have ended the same anyway.

BEYOND SICKNESS AND HEALTH

Or *The Rhetoric of Sick*: in common discourse we call someone Bad if he has done something untoward that we ourselves would do only if we thought we *probably* would not get caught – say take a small amount of money not belonging to us. We call those Sick who have done something so disgusting that we would not do it even if we *knew* we would not get caught – say child rape or other-options-for-food cannibalism. This sort of naming does not result from precise thinking but it is indeed what most do.

A surer way of making our notions clear would be not to think in terms of Sickness and Health only but to employ three terms to cover aberrant behavior: *Sick* and *Error* and *Bad*. One might draw parallels with the three puberties: Biological and Intellectual and Spiritual.

We are familiar with the first sort since almost all of us have entered it and quite a few have gone through it: those who have not so proceeded have not learned that there is a (generally reproductive) purpose for sexuality. These people are called Libertines.

Then there is Intellectual Puberty. Many never enter it though most who do enter manage to pass through fairly quickly, certainly by age thirty. Except for a few late starters, who are not always sad cases. Those others who enter but do not emerge fail to learn that although one's ideas can be played with, generally they are there to Organize a Culture by means of a Set of Lies Commonly Agreed Upon. Those who keep playing with them are called Intellectuals.

The third or Spiritually Pubescent group has difficulty in finding applications to or acting upon revelations: they decline to accept what is freely before them. If just outside Heaven's Gates there were a Discussion Group gathered to hack over the Concept of Heaven they would prefer to go there instead of on to Heaven and perhaps they would prefer to stay there outside. These people tend to enter some aspect of Organized Liberal Religion. Or teach it.

One might look on Aberrant Behavior similarly: those whose oddities are caused by Biological disorders (brain tumors or unbalanced blood chemistry) might well be called Sick. Those whose oddities are based on Intellectual Foibles (Marxists, for example) could be said to be in Error. And those who know better spiritually but persist in such acts they know to be wicked should be called Bad.

Those who refuse this categorization (that is, most modern folk) in favor of calling Sick all those whose behavior is repugnant do so from one Premise and it has nothing at all to do with Science: the premise is that there is no God. That is, of the Theist sort – prior to, separate from and interfering in His creation. Perhaps Science grew up in the formerly Theistic West because man sees himself separate from this world – Cf. Adam and Eve, who got to name the animals *et al* – and thus have an Archimedean point from which to view it: that which is at the other end of the microscope is not us.

But no matter: if there is no separate deity then All is One. Which means that in any given option there will *be* no option, but rather will there be One Way. That which is in accord with the One. And who will perceive this?

The Intelligent Man who is also the Educated Man will perceive it.

But what if there is one who is both Intelligent and Educated who does not agree with this course? He cannot be in Error for there is no possibility for Error in the Truly Educated Intelligence. He cannot be called Bad since such implies at least two options, and thus the issue of Choice enters; this Choice could be based on selecting the intellectually better/best as well as the morally better/best. But if there is but One Way there is no option.

Thus in this system anyone who though Intelligent and Educated still perversely persists in folly can only be called Sick. This is why in the former Soviet Union people who were Intelligent and Educated who did not agree with the Party were sent not so often to the Gulag and Forced Labor but to Psychiatric Hospitals: they were Sick. With the medicines there applied they truly became so. Such happens still in other places.

Marxism has pantheist theology of the Materialist sort [there also is Spiritual pantheism, e.g. Christian Science], which pantheism is the chief form of Atheism (anti-Theism) although there also is Dualism, which posits two deities – unlike the One of Theism and the deity-*is*-all of pantheism. In its most common form it sees Matter and Mind as eternally separate although in all Dualistic systems the Good God always wins (or is projected to do so shortly). Thus Dualism may be said to be pantheism trying to realize itself. Since Dualism is incipiently pantheistic it is the lesser Atheism.

The only other theological alternative is Pluralism which says there are concurrent and possibly unconnected realities. This option may be contradicted by the certainties of Science (unless these certainties constitute only one of the lesser worlds) and anyway it may as well be discarded as an option since if it be true then nothing of any value may be of human certainty.

One other option exists to explain aberrant behavior: Possession, an alternative that can exist only under Theism where not only is visible creation free to choose but so is the invisible.

XVI

Since it was payday Saturday he put on his .45 to go get the money with which to pay the troops and fetched out of his bottom drawer a cardboard box for the Fund Drive money. He didn't know what the Cause would be that he was to collect for that day but there was always something. He set it out next to a card table in the Day Room where they soon would be lining up and pulled up a chair and then went off to get the money.

Grisby advanced it in a single bundle from among several piles he had collected on his desk: these were the francs bought at something like 500:1 which he would sell at the official 350:1 to the innocent. No not innocent:

ignorant. When he got back they were lined up and waiting. They saluted took their pay and gave a portion for charity. Invariably they smiled at him as they did so: as if he cared. It was ridiculous for thirty-five year old men to be afraid of him yet he was aware that many of the Sergeants were just that.

When he took back what was left over Grisby thanked him and kept it separate and when occasion allowed slipped it into a drawer on his desk. Say JP how about that trip to Paris? Jan has to be on duty this weekend and since we're marrying soon (as you know) this may be my last chance: you know all the spots so how about taking me there?

This was the first exchange between Grisby and him since the discovery of Gooley on the pot so it would be a good thing to pick up the opportunity. He said OK they could leave after lunch. Grisby said they would drive: You ought to get a car yourself JP.

I ordered one he said With my uh earnings. Grisby nodded. A sports car he said and left. And ran into Chaplain (Major) Ratty who had gone to payroll to get his own nickels. They walked out the door together he holding it for the Chaplain then falling in on the Chaplain's left. He said he had just learned that Grisby was marrying Jan and the Chaplain said yes to that: he had in fact some papers for Lieutenant Grisby to sign regarding the religious upbringing of the children. Simon said he would have done that for her sake.

Ratty stopped short: You? He nodded. Then why did you free Cholmondelay after he raped her? He said because Cholmondelay didn't rape her. Indeed he did said Ratty: I visited her in the Hospital before arranging for her to go elsewhere. And I can assure you she was raped. And she identified her assailant. I'll be at the bottom of it yet why Colonel Mousse ended it. Or would have been had not the marriage with Lieutenant Grisby been arranged.

Does Grisby know?

He does not. And you are not to tell him. Now if you will accompany me on the way to see the Colonel perhaps we can get to the bottom of this now. He turned them toward Headquarters. In front of that building some workmen were filling in a dug-out hole with sand preparatory to planting a large fir tree that waited even then on the flatbed of a truck parked nearby:

the Colonel wanted it for Christmas decorations in season and as he joked to spruce up the place.

Ridiculous. Everything was ridiculous. And Shaw was wrong: he had not chosen. He had not even known. Jan Gooley and not Marianne?

I saw her in bed with Grisby he said. When Ratty said nothing Simon halted: She's pregnant by Cholmondelay and you wanted Grisby to think it was his.

Ratty resumed his progress. She may or may not be pregnant: but it's an imperfect world. And if she is pregnant it's not the child's fault.

And the situation calls for a bit of deception?

The priest drew in breath and said All Ethics are resolved *in situ* which does not mean Situationism. Situationists err when they say we come to act with nothing prior but a Commitment to Love. To want what is Best for Others. We come with our languages and the assumptions native to it. With our Culture. All of that affects how we decide *in situ*. We want what is *spiritually* best for others. Hitler wanted the best thing for his victims. So did Stalin for his. We say Love God and What you Want Do. We know what God would have us do: what His laws are. Gnostics separate Law from Love. Without God's Laws you get the Ethics of Adjustment. In Hell one Adjusts. And why not if there are no Absolutes and No Way Out? Those are the Ethics of Hell. We are there.

Ratty told the Colonel's secretary that they would like to see her boss and she smiled and sent them in. Inside they didn't see Mousse but incredibly on the desk was Cholmondelay squatting with his trousers down finishing the last of a large and steaming crap. He hopped off the desk and turned while stuffing in his shirt and pulling up his trousers.

You stand right where you are Ratty commanded. Cholmondelay reached into his pocket for a razor and gave the same order to the Chaplain. Then he saw the .45 at Simon's hip and turned and jumped through an open window and out just as Mousse came in behind them shouting. Simon had forgotten about his .45 until Cholmondelay saw it. Then he ran to the window and saw where Cholmondelay had gone and climbed out after him leaving Ratty to explain.

Cholmondelay had run around past the tree being lowered into the hole and was standing under the flag pole: he had taken a hostage and was holding his razor to her throat. It was Queenie Compson. Longbow had been standing with her but was surprised and now was not close enough to do anything to help her. He had seen Simon's .45 though and was retreating toward it.

Then from behind the tree came Shaw like a berserk Viking waving his arms and rushing the pair: Repent he said Before it is too late: Repent!

Suddenly it was too late for Queenie as Cholmondelay drew the razor from one side to the other. He slashed at Shaw who fell back. Then as in a dream Longbow took Simon's .45 and fired: the ball punched through Cholmondelay's chest and spun him around and laid him face down some feet in back of where he had been standing. A large red hole big enough to hide a football in showed then with parts of his spine revealed at the top and bottom of it. Longbow came back to Simon's side and returned the .45.

Then came Mousse and Ratty at full tilt from Headquarters. Both inspected the dead and Shaw who with bloodied hands held his side. Then Mousse after saying Icky Poo left to shake Simon's hand while Ratty knelt before Queenie then moved on to Cholmondelay.

Longbow told him to holster his weapon. Mousse was telling Longbow Simon would get a medal: a commendation for the tree. The Colonel pointed at the Christmas tree but it was a few seconds before Simon realized he was being credited with having suggested it. A Commendation Ribbon the Colonel told him. Sirens were blowing then as the Air Police and Medics came on their way. They couldn't do much except take testimony which he and others gave them and after pictures were made the bodies were carted away. He was through. The Colonel said And maybe another medal for shooting that bastard.

On the fringe of the crowd was Grisby. Lunch JP?

Sure he said then we'll go on to Paris. No reason not to. He suggested to Grisby that they ask Longbow to come along. Grisby said OK but Longbow declined: he was checking out Hoop that day. Final check. Thanks anyway: he would go next time. Hoop was there hanging back on the edge of the crowd waiting for Longbow and as usual not speaking. Nervous probably about the coming Check Ride.

BM got his camera and he picked up his easel and they both packed AWOL bags then he stuffed his pipe and they were off in Grisby's new MG. Paid for this I suppose with the surplus of the French franc differential?

Partly. What're you doing with yours?

Same thing. As I said: I ordered a sports car. Austin-Healey. Saved my shekels and paid cash. Grisby was working his jaw: thinking probably of Simon's buying a car a couple of hundred more costly than his own. He explained it to him: I've been in some years more than you Grisby and I have an advantage in longevity pay.

Then you should have had enough capital to buy the francs yourself JP. He turned a corner in Dam Pierre and they were clear of most villages for twenty miles. It was Spring and the trees in bud lining the road looked like those of a number of 19th century painters he could think of. He said he didn't know where to get the francs at so favorable a rate. But that wasn't really it: I didn't want to go into it alone. I think you would have Grisby (you just needed me to do the actual exchanging for you) but I'm not like that: I wanted a partner.

You'll never make it to the top in business JP.

He said he hoped not and settled on his kidneys to enjoy the ride. When he told Grisby about how odd it was actually to see the trees lined up the way all the famous painters had recorded them abruptly they stopped. Who JP? Who?

What painters? You said there were famous paintings of these trees?

Well maybe not of these same trees: but ones like them. You know: see one tree.... But oh Monet certainly and Sisley and uh Pisarro. That enough? It was: Grisby got out and took pictures going both ways. Then he got back in as abruptly as he'd got out and again they were on their way. Tell me about anything else of interest will you JP? That's why you're along.

But you've seen those trees a hundred times. Or I have. You've seen them more than once – a dozen times at least. That was true said Grisby but Simon knew what it meant: he was to tell him what places he ought to photograph in addition to l'Etoile and the Arch.

Well maybe the Bateaux Mouches. We'll take it from there. Grisby said OK.

And so it went. It was a horrible evening. For one thing the Arabs were confused: one man with a camera and the other with an easel? What in hell were they? But by nightfall the appropriate pictures were taken except for the timed shots he wanted to make. They ate at the Embassy which was ghastly and then he persuaded Grisby that the best shots were to be had when it was fully dark and he dragged him to the Opera.

When Grisby realized he was there not just to take a picture of it but actually to go inside and hear it he paled. But he went. It was *Lucia* and the sextet excellent but Grisby slept through that part. Afterward he recovered enough to do the Café de la Paix then across the street to Le Trou. Grisby didn't like it so they went to Harry's which he did. As they went out Rachel Burger and Sergeant Leigh or people who looked like them went in but neither set stared.

Her bags are packed said Grisby: When she gets back to the Base she's off to the States. That's what Cosmo says.

Right said a voice behind them and turning they saw Cosmo himself. He excused himself to direct a couple of men who looked French: they went in Harry's and emerged presently with Leigh between them. They disappeared around a corner. Where's he going asked Grisby.

Saudi Arabia I think said Cosmo: Since that's a one year tour he can finish out whatever he had left here three times as fast. As you said Grisby she will return to the States as soon as she returns to the Base but she needn't hurry with that since she's a civilian. Care to go to Les Halles? Frantic behind them came out Rachel once again with hands wringing. But as her mouth opened the three chorused as one voice What Does It Mean? This deflated her though she told them to wait there a minute while she went after her purse.

As soon as she ducked inside they caught a taxi for the meat and produce-handling area and were safely gone before she got back. The soup was good and people there sang from time to time but only Cosmo knew the songs and his voice was terrible. Grisby kept falling asleep so the two of them returned to the Arromanches thence to their beds. Cosmo had met an interesting upper-class Britisher and finding someone on his own level was happy enough to be left behind. They would meet him for lunch at a place called The San Francisco.

Grisby didn't mind going with him to the Church of St. George V and rather enjoyed the scenery. After he learned the German Christians had used it for their Cathedral during the Occupation he wanted to take a picture of it and did. The service was well constructed and the Rector spoke on how things were back in New York: a bit brusque until they learned who he was and after that they could not be nicer.

Cosmo as it happened was in the congregation and the three of them strolled quietly to the restaurant. Across the street was a Maserati show room and they looked in the window for some minutes. Simon was pleased enough to be in the company of people for whom such a purchase was not impossible: Cosmo already had a Jaguar and BM doubtless would become wealthy in due season. In uniform the undiscerning eye could not distinguish them one from another. Nor perhaps as they stood: when they went in the San Francisco they got good seats on a balcony. Cosmo had never been on that level before. Simon explained that it was because he'd never been there with him before and Cosmo snorted. Afterwards they saw a soccer game but only Cosmo knew the rules.

Grisby let him drive back since he was sleepy but he was to be awakened for anything unusual. Well we could make a diversion by Chartres Cathedral. No said Grisby he had enough of that sort of thing with Notre Dame and the Ile de St. Louis and besides they might be having a concert. Indeed that was just what Simon had in mind.

When they got back there was a note on his door for him to call the OD. The OD was Pumpkinseed and he said he'd be right over. On arriving he was told Longbow and Hoop were dead: from the radio they gathered Hoop had caused it in some way by panicking although it was hard to understand because the C-119 was a very forgiving aircraft. Anyway Longbow had gone down with the plane and was quietly swearing competently in French all the while and trying to get it flying properly until the last but Hoop got out though his parachute had not opened. At least the French farmers had seen none open and they had not yet found him: perhaps they wouldn't.

How not?

If he went into a small lake or something. Or a haystack maybe. If he did that last one he just might be alive. What you are supposed to do is take over the lead in the search since you're OK in French and not too many are.

They found Longbow?

I think so. Some anyway. Pumpkinseed knew he liked the fellow and looked away as he said it. I'm sorry to be the one to tell you: it happened yesterday and I guess I forgot you'd been gone since before it happened. Thought everyone knew. Well he had to go. He gave Simon the map and told him to take the jeep and get on with it.

He took two enlisted men with him who had been assigned generally to the detail and one of them drove. The plane was in a field of wheat and mainly in one piece. It was neatly cordoned off and was no longer smoking or dangerous: blackened all over it looked like something left over from a settled war. Air Police were guarding it. Apparently all the surrounding area had been searched and since the trouble began at 5000 feet and the descent was mainly straight down he figured Hoop couldn't be very far away even if he'd jumped immediately.

It was getting dark so they went with flashlights and paced across the small and tidy fields. Now and then a farmer would offer commentary but none had seen Hoop descend. By midnight they were wet to their thighs with dew and very tired. And since the farmers they met earlier had each offered refreshment they had headaches from all they'd drunk. But all the farmers were then long abed and there was no new wine being given them.

Once he thought he saw a bit of cruciform phosphorescence over a hill where some sheep were grazing and he expected to find a gelatinous Hoop depressed in the ground nearby. But it was a couple who disappeared quickly into a Deux Cheveau and drove off: France was becoming Americanized. Or just modernized. At 0200 he called it off till the morning.

Back at the wreckage they had coffee with the APs standing guard and listened to the wind move lightly through the metal. Then he noticed that the fog was rising and the ceiling was very low and not moving: no wind no stars no sky. He asked the AP Sergeant about it. Rats he said.

Already? His legs felt weak.

The Sergeant thought so. He was old over thirty at least and probably knew about such things. The longer Sergeants stayed in the more they intensified: became either Very Good or Very Bad. This one he didn't know.

They waited till dawn then began again and kept at it till noon but they never found him. Several farmers approached him and reported severe psychological damage to their cattle and he directed them to the Legal Department for assistance: but they would have to go to La Beauce Air Base to get it since he carried no forms with him.

When he got back to his BOQ he slept till dinner time when he was awakened by the Wing Adjutant who was on his way home: he stopped to tell him that since he had done such a neat job cleaning up Segal's affairs he was given the same privilege with Hoop and Longbow. This would be in addition to his regular duties of course. Simon protested that he was very busy indeed at Headquarters Squadron and hardly saw how he could do both. The Major agreed but said the Colonel specified him. The keys were left with him.

After dinner he made a cursory run-through and found little of interest in Longbow's room: he had no known heirs anyway according to his records and that would make things simple. Actually anything he saw that he wanted he could himself keep and none would know. He chose among other items a picture of Longbow as a young Cadet standing cockily next to a Piper Trainer: it was as if it was himself he saw staring out.

As for Hoop there were many relations and that could be a royal mess if conflicting claims should be filed by various heirs and assigns. There was nothing in Hoop's stuff anyone with taste would want though. Letters from girls who had written to him were in four stacks: four girls. He ran through them and saw them progress in each instance from formal to friendly and the last ended with words looking forward to meeting him: but then they stopped. Poor Hoop. He would read them more carefully later but probably they should be destroyed. Or returned.

In Hoop's closet there were uniforms and only one civilian suit and it had cowboy fringe on it. In back of them stood a fully clothed Marianne.

PARTHIAN SHOT

Whodunits and Fantasy have but little in common though they do seem to. The first has four rules: (1) there is a Closed Society [say a snowed-in small hotel] and (2) All Clues Are Fairly Given and (3) there are to be No Ringers [late-comers are never It] and (4) One is Guilty and the rest are Innocent [though in real crimes usually there are shadings].

It is similar to Greek Scripture upside down: (1) the One had to be a Jew since Gentiles hadn't read the Book and (2) there were hints throughout Hebrew Scripture [e.g. Ps. 22] and (3) *Before Abraham was* said Jesus *I Am* and (4) One was Innocent and the rest Guilty. The game was to guess who It was before being told: Peter nearly had it at Caesarea Philippi but not quite. They all guessed wrong on Friday and on Sunday they were told.

Fantasy is dissimilar although it also has four tricks: (1) Time Elision and (2) the Double and (3) the Story-Within-the Story and (4) Corruption of Reality by Dream. Actually all Reality *is* corrupted by these four elements: Time and Selfhood and the World Without and the World Within. Reality in Fantasy isn't just Hidden as it is in the Whodunit: rather is it Not Ascertainable.

XVII

At breakfast at the Club the next day he sat with Cosmo and Laufer and Grisby discussing their forthcoming trip to La Rochelle to take their new cars to port for shipment back to the States: they were all getting out together (or in his own case completing his tour) and could all take the trip together. Then Bowwow joined them from another table: he had been reading a book and put it beside his place at the table. Simon noticed for the first time that Bowwow hadn't a mop of hair but rather was his head shaped like a pumpkin turned on its side and it only looked like a lot of hair when really it was a lot of head. Nearby a booth held three pubescent girls telling dirty jokes. One of them he thought was Burger's daughter: she it was who in a fairly good job at a Cockney dialect was telling about a bride who all night kept asking 'Arry 'ow about it? He knew the joke.

Bowwow was asked what the book was and he said it was something by one of the James Boys. Grisby asked whether it was about Frank or Jesse and was told it was *by* one of the James Boys not *about* one of them. Only Cosmo smiled: Henry or William?

Henry said Bowwow: Fiction is hardly my area of expertise but I'm trying to improve myself.

Simon said he did that by going to the opera. But what was the book about?

Americans said Bowwow: American Innocence versus European Experience. Or at least that's what the blurb says: I think it would be better said that it's American Ignorance versus European whatever – Experience might do. But the most intriguing part is a quotation in the introduction in which Eliot is quoted as saying of James that *He had a mind so fine no idea could ever violate it.*

Cosmo nodded. Simon and Grisby looked at each other and the latter shrugged. Simon said he didn't know James or Eliot but would look them up. Fine said Cosmo who then said he had a Fantastic idea Fantastic: what we ought to do is hang flags on the hoods of our cars (or tape them down rather) each of us with a different nationality and then race to La Rochelle. Every town we pass through will applaud us. Not a real race of course: except when there are Frenchmen around. He said he owned a small Union Jack about three by four and he could take that one. Simon should use the French flag. Grisby wanted an American flag and had one. Pity there's no one to hang a German flag on said Cosmo looking at Laufer. Laufer shrugged (it was a new gesture for him and he used it whenever occasion allowed) and he agreed to put one on his Porsche. Bowwow said he would try to find a Welsh one or maybe a Scottish one. He already had a Danish one: would that do? He was told that it would.

Now they were ready to start going home. The world was their oyster.

You know Longbow told me once that some day said Simon That I would be nostalgic about all this. He laughed but no one else did.

Too bad about recent events said Cosmo but Shaw is in Wiesbaden and they may bring him back soon. Not so the Librarian Whatsername?

Compson said Grisby in a knowing way that told he'd known her all right all right.

And Hoop said Laufer: We should remember him. And of course Longbow.

Simon said Segal and they all agreed. Then there was the name no one said. He would have raped our daughters said Grisby finally.

Nostalgia said Cosmo Means homesickness: this is not our home. A cheap emotion nostalgia. I hate it because it has always just gone around the next corner just as you are turning the first corner: but still I feel its presence. Americans feel it more I'm told because we move around so much.

They knew Simon had no home at all and fell momentarily silent. Then Grisby spoke: Speaking of presences don't anybody look now but guess who's coming up in back of us. They looked into the mirror over the bar and there was Rachel Burger only some thirty paces ahead of two APs and coming their way. Her daughter saw her and left by the side door. Rachel stopped when she got to their table and waited. She waited too long and the APs arranged themselves on either side of her. I've found it she said quietly to the four and Cosmo looked up to ask who had lost it. Laufer stared intensely into his porridge and Grisby was keenly interested in his coffee cup.

What it Means she said I've Found What It Means. She waved her hands as before but now she smiled. The Colonel would like to see you said the higher ranking AP: He's waiting now and we're to take you there.

She ignored him and repeated the fact if not the content of her discovery. Laufer whose back was perfectly toward her pushed his chair clear of the table and slightly against her legs and rising palmed his bowl of oatmeal on her head. I've found it she said still radiant as the APs turned her and moved her away still crowned and dripping slightly: I've found it!

That's becoming something of a tradition around here Cosmo said to Laufer.

Laufer nodded: She's joined the Church of Christ Scientist. Or thinks she has. Appropriate enough perhaps. Her husband has resigned you know.

Enough of that said Grisby It's time to leave. Can we all go this afternoon? I promised Jan I'd be back by tomorrow. Laufer said he had a few things to check out at his old office but then he could go. So they agreed to pick him up there after lunch.

Simon went with Grisby for a final PX run before their trip. Of course they would not depart for the Land of the Big PX (or Round Door Knobs) for six weeks more or less but once your car was gone you were as good as gone too said Grisby: without a car you were unreal. Maybe said Simon and proceeded to the perfume counter where he bought a large bottle of Ma Griffe to give Jan for a wedding present. He asked Grisby if he cared to step over to Personal Items and pick out his gift. Surprise me said Grisby.

OK he said and then decided it was time to tell him he'd found Grisby's old girlfriend: I have some news for you. Grisby grunted while kicking at a camel saddle. Um There'll be six of us going to La Rochelle he said:

I found Marianne. Grisby paused only slightly in his kicking and said nothing. What I figure is we'll take her there and throw her in the sea. You know a cast your broad upon the waters sort of thing. You're getting married: you won't want her any more. Grisby still looking down thought on it and agreed.

We'll have to tell the others of course. Bowwow knows but the rest don't.

Blame it on Hoop said Grisby: He won't tell anyone.

He thought about that then said OK.

After lunch they found Cosmo at the Chaplain's Office confessing something or other to Laufer's replacement. Laufer wasn't there or at least was not visible: The thing is said the new man Did you love the sheep? That's what's important.

No Mister Bland said Cosmo It's not that simple. Oh it is said Bland It is.

It's time said Simon sticking his head in and Cosmo got up from his chair. Another time he said to the priest who was a mild and sophisticated smiling man and to Simon Where's Laufer?

Outside yelled Laufer Trying to keep from throwing up.

They went out and taped down the flags. While doing so a new man came by with no cross over his left breast pocket but a set of small tablets with a small star over them. He picked out Simon to smile to and was smiled back at in return. The rabbi went inside and they finished taping: an Austin-Healey with a French flag and an MG with an American one didn't seem right but they doubted if anyone would notice. Bowwow had an Aston-Martin. Laufer drove a Beemer and Cosmo his Jag

Tell us said Grisby Was it a ram or a ewe?

You know said Cosmo It was the most amazing thing: the fellow didn't even ask! Laufer only laughed grimly.

Then Grisby and Simon explained to Laufer and Cosmo about Marianne. Or explained part of it. Laufer took it in and excused himself and went back in his former office and returned with a small book and a package: Prayer Stole he said For the Burial Office.

And so they were off and running on a perfect Spring day and at each crossroads town they roared through at more than the speed they'd maintained on the open highway: without fail the local Gendarme would wave them on with one rapidly agitated arm while the other stopped the rest of the world. People cheered and had something to talk about that evening.

On the road they raced only when overtaking by passing another car or truck or when they met one coming from the other direction. Simon got the most applause except once when he was in fourth place they swore at him he was pretty sure for not upholding the honor of France but the curses though shouted were lost in the engine's roar and the dust of the road.

Marianne rode in the trunk of Cosmo's Jaguar since he had the most room. It would not have seemed authentic for her to be seen riding alongside anyone. Besides: what would they do with her when they stopped for dinner?

They fed quite well on gelatined meat and then had langouste with the usual asides. The inn was a low and authentically half-timbered place with cool graveled walks and close-cropped grass. Inside was a piano no one played but it looked as if someone had just stepped aside from doing so. The wall pictures were in the late 1920s fashion: they made it seem as if the pianist who had left had done so thirty years earlier but would momentarily return to discover he had missed a Depression WW2 holocausts atomic bombs Korea Dien Bien Phu and all that. But the music would go on anon.

It was dark when they got to La Rochelle but after checking in their rooms decided night burial might be best. Marianne was weighed with a jack inserted into her derrière with a kick by Grisby: he had it left over as a spare from his other car and it wouldn't do for the MG so it was dispensable. And so they drove to a promontory and carried her the four of them to the edge with Bowwow leading the way and Laufer piously trailing closely.

There they set her down while Laufer vested and then began intoning about commending the soul of their sister departed and committing her body to the deep in the sure and certain hope and all that. Expecting presently the sea to give up her dead when the corruptible bodies of those who sleep shall be changed and made into glorious bodies and so on.

Grisby grumbled that her body was pretty well made as was but they quieted him and they then began to swing her to and fro: with each swing the *to* went a bit farther before it stopped. Then Cosmo said Now and the *to* movement continued and Marianne arc'd up and then went feet first into the sea. Simon paused then threw his pipe after her.

They returned to their Auberge for a night cap.

The TV was on to a Paris station where a soulful chap was singing Dis-Donc Dis-Donc which wasn't too bad if you didn't fully understand it. Then with the news came the announcement that General DeGaulle was again at the helm: it had happened earlier in the day but it was news to them if not to others in the room. They would be leaving in a few weeks and it mattered little anyway.

After dinner Cosmo took Simon aside and said he was worried about Grisby or rather was worried *for* Grisby: it seemed that Jan Gooley had the bizarre custom of bedding enlisted men. She'd go off base with a different one every Wednesday to a nearby Auberge. They came to having a room reserved for her he said And the invariably dark hued man of her choice.

Simon focused on the enlisted part since it was illegal. Cosmo nodded: She forgot that the APs always saw her when they left the base of course and the Office of Special Investigations got hold of it and the lid was about to blow when the Cholmondelay thing happened. Officers aren't supposed to do Enlisted said Cosmo: he was worried for what Grisby was facing. Whoring he said Does not stop at the waist. Of course he said We will not a word of it to Grisby. Simon agreed to that.

And so they went severally to bed: the next day they would have to take their cars to the Port for shipment to the States. For military personnel it was free and was a pleasant perquisite. Grisby was already asleep when Simon put his head to pillow and in the next room he could hear Cosmo talking of how the place had once been a Protestant stronghold. And so he slept. In dreams there came scattered pictures and among them threaded a green-eyed red-haired woman sinking deeper each time until at last she disappeared.

When he awoke in the morning he was a long time remembering who he was and where.

SING WE ONE SING WE TWO SING WE THREE

Between trains in Portland I called a friend
from Air Force days. No! You came by puff-puff!
Say, recall Simon in Nouasseur? Rough
tale to tell, Gris: shot down over Nam. Trend
(Black guy) stayed in, Major at Willow Bend
now – that time at Officers' Call.... Enough
chit-chat: stay the night? Your wife's kind. No, tough
trip ahead. He has a child. I intend
to marry some day. He's in stocks and bonds.
I'm not. J'sais pas. C'est quoi Capital Gain?
Once we could suspend differences, planned
en groupe low-level raids on Paris. Rain
returns us there. Train time. We will disband
now. We won't exchange Christmas cards again.

Made in the USA
Charleston, SC
26 January 2013